Losing a Parent

Losing a Parent

Practical Help for You and Other Family Members

— FIONA MARSHALL —

FISHER
BOOKS

Library of Congress Cataloging-in-Publication Data
Marshall, Fiona
    Losing a parent : practical help for
    you and other family members /
    Fiona Marshall.
        p. cm.
    Originally published: London :
    Sheldon Press, 1993.
    Includes bibliographical references
    and index.
    ISBN 1-55561-223-7
    1. Bereavement—Psychological
    aspects. 2. Grief. 3. Death—
    Psychological aspects. 4. Parents—
    Death—Psychology. 5. Terminally
    ill—Psychology. I. Title

    BF575.G7 M37 2000
    155.9'37—dc21   99-088893

Fisher Books is a member of the Perseus Books Group.

Find us on the World Wide Web at http://www.fisherbooks.com

Fisher Books are available at special discounts for bulk purchases in the U.S. by corporations, institutions, and other organizations. For more information, please contact the Special Markets Department at the Perseus Books Group, 11 Cambridge Center, Cambridge, MA 02142, or call (617) 252-5298.

---

12 13 14 15 — 03 02

Contents

Acknowledgments

First and foremost, my thanks to Peter Cheevers, who made many valuable contributions to this book and who was unstinting in his support.

My thanks also to the people who shared their experiences and time with me, including the Reverend Ian Ainsworth-Smith, Alan Davidson, Mick Smith, Christopher Wood, Hazel Sternberg, Dr. Richard Lamerton, Dr. Emanuel Lewis, Margaret Murray, Henrietta Regan and John Petherbridge.

Thanks also to the Lisa Sainsbury Foundation and the Center for Policy on Aging for generous access to their written materials.

Introduction

WE TEND TO BELIEVE THAT our mother and father will never die. Even if a long illness gives us time to prepare ourselves, we can never be completely ready for their death and its aftermath. No matter what our age, the death of a parent is devastating; nothing leaves us feeling so abandoned. It means saying goodbye to the people who gave us life. Not only do we lose a loved one, we also face a severe identity crisis because that person was so much a part of ourselves and our past.

Our mother's or father's death is often our first close encounter with death and means coming to terms with our own mortality in a very real sense. Life as we have known it stops and we are left in the deep isolation of grief. We must work through this grief—there are no shortcuts to emotional health.

This grief work, which can take years, covers many aspects of our lives. We have to consider our parent's life in a totally new light—to accept him or her as vulnerable, to assimilate this loss of a part of ourselves and to formulate some concept of death.

The need to find meaning in what has happened can transform pain into valuable insights with which to face the rest of our lives. This book explains how to find this meaning, how to see, eventually, your mother's or father's death as the beginning of a new strength and maturity.

The loss of a mother or father is one of society's invisible areas—or, at least, semivisible ones. Like disabled people and struggling young mothers, dying parents have always been around, but they blend into the background, unless you happen to be one of them or closely connected with one of them. The general attitude seems to be that, although it is agonizing, the loss of a parent is more or less expected.

Condolences may skim over the profound psychological effects this event can have. After all, you're an adult, aren't you? This indifferent attitude can accentuate the isolation that is a normal feature of bereavement.

Thanks to media coverage of disasters and post-traumatic stress, the public is more aware today of the damage unresolved grief can cause. More and more people are joining grief support groups; many come to discuss the death of their mother or father. Others come to discuss the loss of a partner and discover they really need to talk about the unabsorbed earlier loss of a parent.

Letting go takes time, and it's possible that you may never completely let go.

Could it be a comment on our culture, which puts so much emphasis on couples, that so many bereavement studies are done on the widowed? In comparison, studies rarely address the death of a parent and its effects on the adult child. Add to this our society's taboo on death and you realize that a person who loses a father or mother may be very lonely indeed.

I hope this book will go some way toward helping if not curing that loneliness. Those who read it will know at least that it is a *shared* loneliness. Having been through the event myself, I appreciate not only this isolation, but the need of a bereaved person to make sense of what has happened. Grieving can be a long process, especially if you need to formulate some personal philosophy of death incorporating both parents, dead or alive, into the framework of a reasonably happy and mature life.

Generally, the younger you are, the harder you will take the death of a parent. But many factors affect grieving: If you are deeply involved in other life events, such as getting married or having a baby, mourning may be delayed or complicated. If you are older and used to having your parents around, perhaps even taking care of them, their loss can be a blow that turns your life upside down. It is by no means uncommon for people age sixty or older to feel like orphans, alone in the world.

Nevertheless, the death of your mother or father is part of the natural sequence of events. Parents do usually die before their children. In some ways, their death also frees their adult children to take on responsibilities and roles they might not have accepted before the death. The bereaved gain mentally, culturally and perhaps materially from the loss. Although frightening, the challenge of dealing with loss can be liberating.

While the primary emphasis of this book is on growth and recovery, remember that meaning cannot be forced or rushed. Death cannot always be mentally cleaned up with all the coping strategies that come to us from religion and other sources. Letting go of what has happened is a vital part of recovery, with its pain, its raggedness and its imperfection.

The ambulance that didn't come in time, the doctor who was casual, the priest who was less than comforting—these may always hurt, but you can't hold on to them if you ever want to feel whole again. Letting go takes time, and you may never completely let go. No one will ever be at ease with the way Dad died, or see it as neatly fitting in with the universe's master plan.

Pain and grief may have an ultimate value. This value, however, is not easy to acquire. When we try to make sense of what has happened, we always risk frustration.

The way you go through any bereavement also depends on the quality of your relationship with the person who died. A completely smooth parent-child relationship is hard to find and a certain amount of intergenerational conflict is inevitable, even healthy. But death, which may not have left you time to resolve some things in the relationship with your parent, does not necessarily end this relationship.

Ideally, as the years go by, you will have enough time to reach a greater understanding of your mother or father. This understanding includes more acceptance of the way they lived as well as the way they died.

How This Book Is Arranged

Everyone's experience is different, but by including a number of case histories, I hope that this book will touch on as many different reactions as possible. I interviewed people from a wide range of ages and social backgrounds.

It is all too easy for an author to hide behind bereavement jargon, which doesn't really help a grieving person and can even add to her feeling of bewilderment. For this reason, I deliberately avoid using psychological terms such as *searching* (a reaction shortly after death that involves going around the house looking for or expecting to see the dead person).

Because many parents today die of one kind of lingering disease or another, this book opens with what is really the beginning of death: hearing the news or realizing that your mother or father is dying. Next, I consider death itself, with a separate section on sudden death, which can cause a different reaction than other forms of death cause, including a greater sense of shock.

Then I examine grief in great detail, from immediate grief, covering the first two years, to the factors that can complicate or prolong grief. It is important to look beyond this, however, to the process of working through grief and the life that follows.

The grief of losing a parent isn't unique only because parental influences have a way of haunting us for life; we may miss our parent in more situations and for a lot longer than we expect to. As we continue to mature, the death of our mother or father pushes us to come to terms with our grief.

1

Terminal Illness: Anticipating Death

H EATHER, A THIRTY-YEAR-OLD BANK CASHIER, waited all day for her mother, Barbara, to return from the hospital where her father was suffering from bowel cancer. Barbara returned at last in the late afternoon.

> ✺ "She asked me to make her a cup of coffee, which I thought was strange because she always made her own. When it was ready, she sat down. She told me that my father's operation was over. I asked how he was and she said he was weak. Then she said that the surgeon had spoken with her. The doctors had opened him up and then sewed him up again because they saw that his cancer was inoperable. The doctor said it was only a matter of a couple months now."

Nothing can soften the shock of hearing that your mother or father is dying. Even if you already had your suspicions, another person's voice confirming your private fears can feel like an intrusion—even a violation. There is a long-established hatred for the bearer of bad news, the messenger of doom. When the news is broken to you, this hatred can become very real—even when whoever tells you tries to be tactful and kind.

Nothing can soften the shock of hearing that your mother or father is dying.

Doctors are used to dealing with anger from relatives of a dying person. Depending on the circumstances, you may hear the news from someone in the medical profession. If one or both of your parents are failing and elderly, the doctors will consider you the most appropriate person to tell.

You may hear about your parent's condition from another family member, often your other parent. Thus, you also experience the shock of seeing family members break down—an unshakable aunt in tears, a loud-mouthed brother silenced. Worst of all is the reaction of your other parent.

Until now, he or she may have seemed untouchable, with familiar strengths and weaknesses. Now, familiarity is destroyed, roles break down and disorientation sets in. Life enters a strange state of suspension that consists of waiting for death. This is a terrible time during which you may experience the range of reactions from peace to searing pain.

For now, your body will probably respond before your mind does. Your most immediate reaction on hearing the news can produce real physical symptoms similar to those of a cold: clammy hands; feelings of heaviness, giddiness and sickness; the need to go to the bathroom often or sudden diarrhea. You can help move this shock along by keeping warm and quiet, and drinking hot fluids, preferably nonalcoholic and noncaffeinated. It may seem trivial even to think of these things at such a moment, but for many reasons it is essential to take care of yourself from the start of this experience.

In the first place, obvious as it may sound, you have to go on living.

In the first place, obvious as it may sound, you have to go on living. You will not function well unless you make a conscious effort to eat and sleep well during the extremely stressful time that lies ahead. As you will see later, bereavement is a prime time for sickness to strike because the stress of grieving lowers your resistance to infection.

Physical illness is not only debilitating in itself, it also paves the way for prolonged, negative mental reactions. Depression is one example, whether it's post-flu blues or the washed-out feeling that comes after a stomach bug. An overall gloomy outlook can be another reaction.

If, for example, you have neglected to eat well for several months and have lost weight, you may see yourself as skeletal and unhealthy. Anorexia could develop in this situation, or you may just feel unattractive and not worth bothering with.

Generally, if your parent dies of some disease, you are likely to be more anxious about any illness that strikes you, and you may make a bigger deal about it than necessary. Taking care of yourself helps to protect you from such exaggerated long-term reactions, although most grieving people will be touched by them to some degree. It is normal to feel a confusing range of emotions.

It is normal to feel a confusing range of emotions.

Also, you need to be strong to support your parent and other family members if necessary. To be strong, you must know when to stop and relax. People outside a family in which a parent is dying, and sometimes the dying parents themselves, are sometimes hurt and shocked when the children take time off. The children may spend a day in the country or an evening at the movies, apparently forgetting all about their parents' plight. But taking this time away is necessary and nothing to be ashamed of.

Following the initial shock, disbelief may set in, the conviction that the doctor made a mistake or that your father will show his usual strength of character and pull through. You may think the doctor is wrong because he or she doesn't know your father as well as you do or because you simply feel it's not time for your parent to die.

This feeling is what makes losing a mother or father different from other losses: the childish conviction that they are betraying their responsibility as your caretakers by dying. No matter how mature you are, try to come to terms with this in yourself, because it will save you from later anger at your selfishness.

After disbelief has passed (although it may flood in periodically for a long time after the initial shock), other reactions begin to surface. Anger, a common part of bereavement, can take unexpected and disturbing forms. You may direct your anger not only at the perceived incompetence of doctors, or at God, but also at your parent for dying. This anger can be especially intense if you have some important event coming up, such as a new job.

You may start trying to control the event in your head, wanting your father to wait for a marriage, the birth of a child or for just a few more months of life. At the same time, you may also wish death would come quickly. This terrible waiting, during which you want to hang on to your father *and* speed him on his way, can be a time of great confusion.

You may be angry with your mother for imposing or allowing your father's fatal lifestyle—for not making him give up smoking or drinking or simply for not taking care of him.

> ⁊ Michael was a thirty-five-year-old mechanic whose mother spent several months in her native country every year. He thought that his father, Tom, who was seventy-two, was dying partly because his mother hadn't been around to take proper care of him. Good food and prompt medical attention might have given Tom a few more years of life—had Michael's mother been there to take care of him.

This anger at the other parent, complicated by guilt over the dying parent's grief, is very real, however irrational. All you can do is be aware of it but try not to let it get you down. It will pass.

You may also have to cope not just with your own reactions but with those of siblings or other family members. As you will read later, this is a great time for family discord. All those buried childhood resentments rise, you forget to treat siblings as adults, or other family members treat you as a child.

> ⁊ Michael had a difficult relationship with his three older brothers. He felt the oldest two never gave him any respect, and that the other one despised him. The brothers had little in common and, as their father was dying, they quarrelled.

Generally, having to deal as an adult with an event that can easily return you to child status causes tension. Of course, not everyone experiences this kind of upheaval; some families cope better than others. Depending on the maturity of the individual members and their relationships, they may work together all the way through their shared experience.

> ⌒ Stephen, with his two brothers and one sister, shared the responsibilities brought about by his mother's death in a practical, trouble-free way. "It was a terrible time, but we all felt we just had to get on with it. There was no tension among us."

You may feel relieved, especially if your parent has been ailing for a long time. To give up your own struggles with hope, to know that his suffering will end, makes this relief undeniable. Deep down, the exciting thought of true independence may also surface. "Now at last I'll be able to see what it's like to be on my own."

You may feel relieved, especially if your parent has been ailing for a long time.

Naturally, such a feeling is likely to open the floodgates for the guilt of a lifetime. All the neglected opportunities, all the parental love that wasn't quite returned, all the times you were angry with your parent in the past and all the times you and your brothers and sisters may have rebelled against parental authority can flow in. The natural ambivalence involved in the parent-child relationship makes this guilt strong and lasting.

Fear is one of the most isolating and draining emotions of this time, although this partly depends on how much prior experience you have had with death. Someone who has had to cope with the death of a grandparent—or an aunt, uncle or family pet—is better prepared for the reality of death, although this doesn't take away the intense emotional reactions.

A parent's death may seem like the beginning of your own death, the first pull of yourself toward that great darkness. It strikes home with real force: "If they can die, then so can I!" You have to work through the implications of this for a long time during bereavement.

In addition to this basic fear, you may also be afraid of being with your dying mother or of being present at the moment of

death and afterward. These fears are natural in a society of
individuals who have little experience with death. Even if you
have had experience with other family members who died, a
mother or father is closer to home in every sense.

You may not have seen the body of your grandmother who
died when you were twenty, but you are now faced with the
possibility of being with your mother in her last moments. As with
all fear, though, thinking about it is often more unpleasant than the
actual experience. Being present at death can actually be a source
of peace and relief. (See chapter 3 for more about the moment
of death.)

Your feelings, although strong, are not always easy to identify:
You may feel confused or simply blank. Be gentle with yourself;
unfortunately, there is no shortcut through the trauma of grief.
Grief is not an illness, but you must deal with it to grow and
find peace.

Telling: Who Tells Whom about Imminent Death

How the news of imminent death is broken can reveal a family's
lifelong habits and relationships, and can have far-reaching
repercussions. It touches on the core of the parent-child
relationship—whether trusting, evasive, calm or conflict-ridden—
and is a major test of communication within the family.

> ⵣ Guy, twenty-one, knew his father was ill but not
> how seriously. Because he was taking his final
> exams at college, his family felt he should be
> shielded from the reality of his father's cancer. His
> aunt, who strongly disagreed, took matters into her
> own hands and called Guy to tell him the truth.
>
> Guy came home to find that the doctors had
> just given his father three weeks to live. This proved
> correct almost to the day and left Guy very little time
> to accept the news or prepare for the event. Guy
> was angry with his family for protecting him this
> way. Although he was technically adult, he was still
> being considered too young to know.

Guy's story highlights one aspect of a father's or mother's death—the sense of being left out when the older members of the family decide to keep the news to themselves. Guy found these adult lies even more frustrating because the hospital staff could have offered frankness, as well as support and counseling.

After his father's death, he found it even harder to offer support to his mother because she continued her previous lack of openness by bottling up her feelings and not confiding in him at all. His mother's method of "telling" also caused Guy to re-examine his parents' values and his relationship with them. He concluded there was a history of noncommunication and too much emphasis on academic success. He had been told too little all his life.

The right way to be told

Ultimately, there is no *right* way to break the news of death. Sometimes, depending on intrafamily relationships, the news does not need telling. Death is there for all to see. Words are unnecessary.

What role does the doctor (and staff) play when it's time to break the news that someone is dying? Today's hospital personnel are more frank in the face of death, but there is still a long way to go.

> *Much of telling depends on how willing, or how capable, the listener is to hear.*

In an ideal situation, your hospital will have a team of doctors, nurses, occupational therapists, physiotherapists and counselors. The team will have regular meetings and at some point they'll decide that a patient's disease is incurable. Then they'll decide how to tell the sick person and his family. In this way, you can be sure that any news is given in a thorough, sensitive manner.

In smaller organizations, the individual doctor on duty determines how and how much you are told. Even in large hospitals with a well-organized team, there is no best or recognized way of breaking this news because so much depends on the nature of each dying person.

In theory, most professionals agree that the sick person *should* be told first, and then the family, but it is difficult to tell the truth to someone who constantly denies she is ill and insists she is getting better. Much of telling depends on how willing, or how capable, the listener is to hear. Sometimes, even with the best efforts, it is impossible for a dying person or her relatives to believe the news.

Also, the doctor may be clumsy in her telling. Although doctors get some training in death counseling, they may not put it into practice and can easily get overwhelmed by the rest of their work. Also, even when a doctor is as clear as possible, it can be easy to mishear or misunderstand what she is saying.

A doctor may say, "Things don't look good but there is always something we can do." The doctor believes she has imparted the news of impending death. You leave thinking that a cure is possible, but the doctor was really talking in terms of making the sick person more comfortable during his last weeks.

Getting information about your parent's condition can be more difficult if your parents have been told but aren't willing to tell you. The doctor has done her duty and, like the rest of her team, is probably too busy to look for someone else in the family who might need help.

If you are confused, or if you fear the worst but can't get straight answers from your family, ask someone else for help. Probably the best person to ask would be the hospital chaplain.

Ethically, of course, he cannot divulge private information about a patient, but he might be able to advise you on how to break a communication barrier with your parents or the doctor.

Treatment and Relationships with the Medical Profession

It is easy to misunderstand what medical treatment your parent is receiving. Doctors are used to hearing conflicting messages from the relatives of a dying person who are unable to bear the fact that death is coming in its own way, in its own time.

"Can't you give him something to speed it up?" may be followed hours or even minutes later by, "Why haven't you tried something that would give him a few more comfortable months?"

It's a time of great confusion: waiting for the end, wanting it to be over, yet desperately hanging on to your parent for as long as possible. Not only is it hard to accept our own lack of authority in the face of death, but it is also possible to view the doctor as a substitute parent or authority figure. This makes it harder to accept that the doctor doesn't have the answer.

Hospital routines can also make it difficult to keep up with what is going on. Doctors and nurses change shifts and a patient's condition sometimes changes quickly, especially if the patient is in intensive care.

> ⨝ Julia was called to the hospital with the news that her father, Martin, was dying. At seventy-seven, Martin had just had a successful operation for cancer of the pancreas, but now Julia and her family were told that drugs to relieve excess water weren't working.
>
> But even as the family received sympathy from the hospital staff, another doctor decided to do more X-rays. He provided a completely different diagnosis and prescribed new drugs—with amazing success. Martin left the hospital two weeks later to recuperate in a nursing home, and he lived another four years.

If you're not sure what's going on in terms of diagnosis and treatment, go back and discuss the situation with the doctors.

Your mother may want to discuss treatment choices with you. Take this opportunity to listen to any fears she has. She may be afraid of being left alone or in pain, of being a burden, of suffering a long drawn-out death or of losing control.

It is worth noting that older people generally have fewer death fears than younger people. They've accomplished more and have fewer plans for the future. If they've been seriously ill before, they may feel they're living on borrowed time, especially if their spouse or friends have already died.

> ⨝ Maria's mother had no fears of death itself— it was the death process she hated, with all its indignities and suffering. She managed to live a fairly full life for some years after her illness was

diagnosed, but recurrent health problems exhausted her. Her family thought she was relieved to die.

You may also feel that the choice of managing your parent's last days is an obvious one.

> ❧ Heather's father was about to die—the cancer had spread throughout his body. He had lost a lot of weight and was almost skeletal. The doctor told Heather's family that he could put her father on an intravenous drip (IV), but that it would only keep him alive for a few days. The family agreed to stop any further treatment. Heather's father was allowed to die this way.

Where to Die?

Consider the practical options offered by a hospital, hospice or home. Many people would prefer to die at home but don't want to burden their families. Not everyone can afford to take time off from work to care for a sick parent, or to pay someone else to do so. Nor is it unusual for families to be scared of the responsibility.

Having a parent die at home is stressful, but those who choose that path often have positive feelings afterward.

Having a parent die at home is stressful, but those who choose that path often have positive feelings afterward. If you have children in the house, including them in the death can be healthy—if *you* are not too anxious. Secrecy troubles children, together with horrible visions in their own minds.

Seeing Grandma in her last moments may take much of the terror of death away. On the other hand, if your parent needs a lot of nursing, or is in pain, you may feel that this is not an experience you want to share with your children. You need to be strong to consider this option, even with the medical support you would have.

Some people are simply too ill to be cared for at home. In addition, a hospital can seem safe and reassuring; nurses and doctors are on call and some patients settle into the ward routine with ease. Patients may make friends with the nurses and doctors and may feel proud of being a good patient.

> ◝ Anita's mother, Yvonne, became the ward pet, someone with whom the nurses always stopped to pass the time of day, and who always managed a witty reply. Although in some ways a difficult and temperamental woman, she did have charm, and Anita felt that the staff was truly saddened when Yvonne died.

A hospice is more likely to include the family in treatment and pain relief. There may be more open acceptance of death; many people have spoken or written about the peaceful, even happy, atmosphere that can exist in a hospice. The extra involvement of hospice staff can be helpful in starting to deal with your grief, and many hospices offer grief support groups (as do some hospitals). Most of all, a hospice offers peace and dignity to your parent, an assurance that to be dying is not to be written off, that life still has value and meaning.

It can be a relief for your mother or father not to be in a hospital, where the emphasis is on curing, but in a place where death is faced openly. This doesn't have to mean a brave, smiling acceptance of death the minute you walk through the door. One of the positive aspects of a hospice, from your parent's point of view, is that he may be more able to get in touch with and express all the feelings of anger, grief and fear that he may have felt obliged to hide until now.

A hospice emphasizes the quality of life until death takes place, with pain control and individual care that often makes it a far more vital time than could have been hoped for. Some hospices even offer help for patients who are living out their last days at home.

Care at Home

Whether or not your parent *dies* at home, there may be times during the course of an illness when she needs to be cared for at home. Giving this care depends on how much help that parent is willing to accept from a child, even when that child is adult. Some parents refuse to let go of their position of authority and may want to oversee the running of the house, directing their care from their beds. Yvonne, for example, would even tell her daughter what brand of laundry detergent to buy.

Home-Care Tips

- Arrange the sickroom for your parent with a special table for books, drinks and medicines.

- Your parent may appreciate new pajamas, especially if she has lost a lot of weight.

- Often, ill people don't want mirrors around—Michael's father asked for his mirror to be taken away because he couldn't bear the sight of himself after losing so much weight.

- The sickroom will probably be a bedroom, but sometimes your parent may need a room on the ground floor or near the bathroom.

- If your other parent has to sleep in a spare bedroom, put a few flowers in there.

- Keep hospital, doctors', advisers' and support group phone numbers on hand.

- Make sure you get time out of the house and share the care with other family members.

- Follow any medical instructions carefully, especially when it comes to pain relief, which may depend on regular doses to be effective.

Nursing your parent requires all the tact, strength and detachment you can come up with. You need to cultivate the awareness of when to offer a drink and when not to, when to speak and when to be silent. Sometimes you will do the wrong thing unintentionally—such as closing the blinds when the sick person wanted them open. This minor oversight may anger your other parent, who can't help taking out his frustration on you.

Nursing your parent requires all the tact, strength and detachment you can come up with.

You also need to help your other parent without being obtrusive, to care for your dying parent while allowing your other parent to maintain his independence. Above all, you need to maintain a balance between the need for normality in your life and the special pressures caused by your parent's sickness.

If you can have some part in this experience, no matter how small, it will give extra purpose to your days with a sick parent at home. With one room designated as sickroom, and nurses and doctors coming and going, the familiar character of the house will change. It is easier if you can accept this and be part of it.

No Admittance?

One of the most frightening aspects of having a sick parent today is the possibility that he or she may not be admitted to the hospital because of bed shortages or insurance guidelines.

> ⳇ Michael had to struggle to get his father into the local hospital, which was about to close. In fact, his father, Tom, was one of the last patients admitted. Michael thought that losing his temper was what got Tom any attention at all—there were too few people on the staff and morale was obviously low.
> Michael's entire hospital experience was filled with pain and indignity, starting with an ambulance driver who expressed doubts about whether the hospital would let Tom in the emergency room.

Stephen experienced the same kind of thoughtlessness when he took a taxi to his father's funeral—the taxi driver wanted to talk all the way about how hardened he was to funerals except when he saw the small white coffin that meant a child. Neither Michael nor Stephen hesitated in shutting up their respective tormentors. Stephen called the local taxi company to complain about their driver's self-admitted lack of feeling, pointing out that the driver's behavior could have been devastating to a more sensitive passenger. There is certainly no need to put up with this kind of conversation silently.

Visiting the Hospital

Seeing your parent in the hospital can be disturbing. It isn't so much the nondescript beds or the sterile cleanliness as the fact that your parent has been taken out of her natural setting. She is at other people's mercy, no longer the authority figure. It's the stripping of dignity that may get to you—seeing your parent connected to tubes, or in pain or distress.

> As Maria put it: "I hated seeing my mother naked—both mentally and physically. It didn't seem right for a mother to lose all her privacy in front of her child."

And Michael, like many others, found it heartbreaking to see his father so afraid in the hospital—partly the fear of being moved from home and partly the fear of death.

> "I remember that my father still had his spirit the last time I saw him at home. But after that awful medical examination, just after he'd been admitted, he came out of the room terrified and kept clinging to me and asking me to stay. He was rolled down the corridor and I knew he didn't want to go. He was fighting every inch of the way. That was the last time I saw him conscious."

Michael's father, a strong-willed man, was not one to accept death lightly in any case; people often die in the same spirit as they lived.

Be wary of the dangers of overempathizing: It's easy to attribute more pain and sensitivity to a parent than is the case.

Your own pain may cloud your objectivity. It can be hard to admit to ourselves that our parent may *want* to go, that his readiness for his death is

> *People often die in the same spirit as they lived.*

different from ours. While no one would deny the real nature of Tom's suffering, Michael later wondered if he hadn't overreacted slightly, whether he'd been projecting his own acute feelings of distress onto his father.

> ⌒ "Maybe he did want to go and it was me who didn't want to admit it. I blame the hospital partly for that: The medical apparatus, the doctors' attitudes, it all seemed to come between us. How can either one of us really tell what the other person is thinking in an atmosphere like that, where the staff is half-pretending they're going to cure him when they don't really care?"

Michael didn't build a rapport with any of the constantly changing and (he felt) indifferent staff of the large and busy hospital. He was also upset with the hospital chaplain, who seemed uncaring, unprofessional and slow to act.

But, as this is a time of such sensitivity, remember that it is hard for anyone to say just the right thing. Every well-meant comment can hurt. A question about your father's religious beliefs or practices can seem a rude and irrelevant intrusion.

It should be noted that Michael, like Tom, was a restless spirit, more ready to pick a fight with his comforters than to accept comfort from them. All unsatisfactory encounters are magnified in the hospital setting, without the familiarity of home, especially if you know your parent will never leave the hospital again.

It helps to talk to someone during this time of waiting. Help may not come automatically; you may have to ask. At this stage, the doctor doesn't have to be the obvious person anymore— perhaps you don't need authoritative knowledge as much as you need someone who understands. (This isn't to say that doctors don't understand, of course!) A doctor *can* help by giving what is often a fairly accurate estimate of how much time remains.

Many people, however, can and do defy the six-months-to-live prophecies. Doctors make closer estimates when it's a question of weeks or days.

You may have made friends with someone who has been around for more time than a doctor—a nurse, a volunteer, another patient or another patient's family. Your father may also have made friends with the staff, who may visit on their own and can share some of your fear and sorrow as death comes closer.

Michael's experience was negative, but many people speak of the dedication and care of the staff members who took care of their parent. Heather experienced sensitivity and tact in her dealings with the hospital team that cared for her father. Maria felt that the hospital personnel were doing their best, often under difficult circumstances.

Other aspects of illness can make hospital visits distressing, such as body odor, which can linger in your memory even after leaving the hospital. Guy, seeing his father in the hospital for the first time in six weeks, was shocked at how much he had changed physically.

> "His face looked bony—it had always been thin, but now you could really see his cheekbones. His breathing was louder. And there was a kind of glaze over his eyes. When he looked at me, it was as if he wasn't really seeing me, as if he couldn't."

This kind of inward viewing becomes more evident the closer death is, when the attention of the sick person turns away from the outer world. It is an unmistakable state, but if you are not prepared for such a change, it can be a shock to realize that your parent is already so far away.

2

You and Your Dying Parent

C AREFULLY RE-EVALUATE YOUR CURRENT relationship with
your dying mother or father in the final months and weeks
of life, as the past and the future rush together with fewer and
fewer possibilities.

How do you behave with your dying mother? Should
oncoming death make such a difference? Isn't it better to act as
normally as possible? Should you try to talk to your mother about
death? These are some of the most difficult questions you will ever
have to face.

Generally, doctors agree that the dying person leads the way
when it comes to talking about death. If he or she isn't willing,
little can be done to initiate an open discussion. Research
has shown that the dying are usually aware of their true
condition—you know for yourself that your body generally
tells the truth about your health.

Feeling weak and ill can be enough evidence for many sick
people, but everyone has the right to limit how much he admits,
even to himself. And while we might agree that it is better to be
open, it depends greatly on your individual relationship with your
mother or father.

> ⊰ As Guy put it: "Knowing my father was dying
> seemed to give me a kind of secret knowledge about
> him—it seemed wrong that I should know when he
> didn't, because he was my father and fathers should
> be more knowledgeable and more powerful than
> their sons.
>
> *(Continued . . .)*

"They'd tried to tell him, but he didn't want to discuss it. I don't remember what we talked about at visiting time, but I know death never entered the conversation. He would barely admit he was ill; he died very quietly. I wish we could have shared our knowledge—I don't mean great in-depth talks, but just a word or two."

Accepting that your father is growing weaker is that much harder if you're not officially supposed to know, and if your mother isn't willing to know either. Acknowledging the truth can be unexpectedly liberating, as well as giving real value to the time that is left. Like Guy, Heather was appalled at the power she felt she was given when she knew her father's actual condition. She tried to hide it from herself and him, and, one visiting day, talked for a while about the vacation they would all take when he was better.

"He listened to me, then said, 'I just don't think I'll be there.' That was the closest he came to admitting he was dying. But it was enough—the truth really hit me between the eyes. Somehow I'd managed to push it away until then. I went home and cried and cried. To be honest, having the pretense destroyed was a relief. After that, visits were much easier and quieter—sadder, too, but I felt like he'd given us permission to be sad."

Sadness has a hundred disguises.

If you can't be sad at such a time, when can you? Letting out the appropriate feelings isn't always as easy as it might seem: Sadness has a hundred disguises. In addition, making sure you display the "right" feelings in front of your mother is a childhood habit that can be hard to break.

To talk openly about death, to reveal emotion, to break down and weep before your mother may feel too selfish, too melodramatic and too painful. It's not just that your parent is too close to you; it's the frightening admission that her power is on the wane and your life structure is crumbling.

It takes courage to plunge into such conversations. There are no easy answers to a comment like the one Heather's father made. It's up to you and your parent, of course, but a person who starts this type of conversation usually doesn't want to be dismissed. In fact, research has proved that parents are usually hurt by a conspiracy of silence and that you may be able to help if you are willing to listen and talk frankly.

Some people value their privacy to the end and feel stronger alone.

You could also ask if there's anything they want done after death, such as writing a letter to a long-lost relative, disposing of clothes in a certain way or making contributions to some charity. Settling such things can help both sides accept what is going on.

What if your parent doesn't unburden herself? Can or should you intrude? Again, one hint or question is enough. If your mother doesn't listen or changes the subject, you have done your best and all you can do is accept that she doesn't want to talk. Some people value their privacy to the end and feel stronger alone.

Personality Changes in Your Parent

Sorting out your relationship with your dying parent will probably be complicated by other factors. First, for some of the time at least, you may not be seeing your parent in his familiar setting, but in a hospital room, with all the paraphernalia of charts and IVs and the intrusion of visiting hours. Also the unfamiliar emotions of other family members can make it difficult to be as simple and natural with your dying parent as you might like.

Last, but not least, are the effects of any illness. Pain, drugs and the knowledge of oncoming death may all alter your father's personality, sometimes leading to uncharacteristic and disturbing manifestations of irrationality and negativity.

      Anita had always confided in her mother, Yvonne, and regarded her as a source of strength during the emotional turmoil she experienced while growing up. In Anita's midtwenties, Yvonne developed a tumor in the brain that made her increasingly confused and dependent on her daughter. Anita was bewildered by the personality changes in her mother, who became both irritable and depressed.

Yvonne constantly found fault with Anita for doing little things wrong, such as putting too much food on her plate. She often exhausted herself by shouting at her daughter. Anita often felt that her mother had already died and she was caring for a stranger inhabiting her shell.

It is hard to deal with anger and bitterness from a much-loved father or mother, to see them degenerate in any way. Memory loss is a painful example of this: While *your* consciousness is sharpening, your mother's is diminishing. As memories grow more precious to you, they fall further and further out of existence for her. Perhaps the hardest part of this kind of mental deterioration, a feature of Alzheimer's disease, is to be constantly giving without ever getting much in return.

It wears down the most persistent good intentions to have your tasks forgotten as soon as they've been performed, to realize that you and your mother are living in different time zones. Perhaps she's reverted to a time in the past, or perhaps she has lost the concepts of past and future altogether, living only in the present—something hard to imagine until you're faced with it. It can become a constant source of stress.

Dealing with petty irritation is one thing; handling more dramatic manifestations of degeneration is another. You may not always be able to cope with tearful, angry outbursts as calmly as you'd like, or to soothe continued restlessness.

This is when it is important to get as much outside help as possible. Try contacting a support group that specializes in your parent's condition (see Useful Addresses at the end of this book).

Certain emotions are a natural part of dying.

It can help to realize that, besides the actual effects of illness or medication, certain emotions are a natural part of dying. Psychological observations of dying people have revealed five normal psychological stages: denial and isolation, anger, bargaining ("Please let me live until my son gets married and I'll behave very well, or I'll give some money to the hospital chapel"), depression and acceptance. The bereaved go through a similar process (see chapter 5).

While this is uncomfortable reading for those experiencing the actual event, it can be reassuring to know that emotional changes are the norm and that they may not come in the form you expect. If you anticipate loving scenes with your dying parent, it can be cruelly disconcerting when, like Anita, you are met with resistance over the most trivial things.

> *Try to accept that changes in your parent have little to do with you personally.*

Try to accept that changes in your parent have little to do with you personally. She has to come to terms with death in her own way.

Some people think they can handle anything as long as their parent's basic personality remains unchanged. It is extraordinary how much courage and humor a dying person can display. You may be amazed at how much they remain themselves.

Nevertheless, in the end you may have to face a growing *absence* of personality, or at least the personality you have known. Your parent is likely to seem increasingly remote as he or she moves further and further away from everyday life.

Many people have shared Anita's feeling that, as death approaches, the soul has already flown even if the body remains. Though sometimes weird to go through, this can take away some of the drama and fear from the actual moment of death. Death can then be experienced as a natural and peaceful ending.

Unfinished Business with Your Parent

Unfinished business is one of those semitechnical terms you see in books on grief and hear grief counselors use. It can be defined as any problems in your relationship with your parent that need to be resolved before death or just anything that needs to be said or worked out.

When tackling this, bear in mind that, with or without beliefs in an afterlife, death does not have to end a relationship. Parental relationships have a way of influencing our lives for many years, whether death has intervened or not.

Taking this longer view can be helpful because you may not be able to finish all the business right now. You may need more time to formulate a different perspective or to gather the life experience that will enable you to understand your parent and yourself better.

On the other hand, you may not be able to improve your relationship any further.

> ꩜ Stephen felt that any business between him and his parents would never have been finished no matter how much time had been available, because he and his parents just didn't communicate.

Again, unfinished business may not be anything clear, like formal apologies for not becoming a lawyer as your parent wished, or for dropping the family religion. You may need to discuss issues before you make amends.

What you and your parent say before death doesn't necessarily sum everything up.

Keep in mind: What you and your parent say before death doesn't necessarily sum everything up. The words of the dying are traditionally deemed to have special meaning and deep personal value, but they are not the end of the story, and they can be out of place.

> ꩜ Maria increased the time she spent taking care of her mother's physical needs while she was at home—combing and cutting her hair, helping her with her colostomy bag, washing her nightgowns.
>
> Maria felt this was a natural process in which she was in some small measure repaying her mother for all the care that she had given to her as a child. Without too many words, Maria and her mother reached a conclusion to their living relationship before her mother's final admission to the hospital.

This is hard if your relationship with your parent has been troubled; problems from childhood achieve their greatest strength now.

> ⁊Michael's father, Tom, a difficult man, had had a convoluted, bitter relationship with the family, especially after a family wedding where he got drunk and caused a scene. The family split into two camps and continued the feud ever since.
>
> Because of this, Michael was naturally even more upset at his father's dying. Also, as the youngest son, Michael felt he had always had to work for his father's approval. He never quite had it, although he felt he supported his father the most, and was most like him in character.

What can you do? As Michael discovered, impending death does not necessarily open everyone's eyes and smooth over all family problems. You cannot shake an obstinate, old father into recognizing the error of his and other people's ways.

The need to make your father or mother recognize what is happening is an attempt to control what death is showing cannot be controlled. Letting go of your parent can help release all the misunderstandings between you and her and all the stubborn beliefs that may have dominated your lives.

This may also involve letting go of how you see your mother, not as she is, but as you would like her to be—more mature, more humane, more able to empathize with you. Disturbing as it may seem, because our parents may have done a lot for us, we have to face the fact that our inner child can always demand more.

Strangely, if your father was distant in life, it is likely you will idealize him in death and forgive his shortcomings. You may say your father was misunderstood or not given enough recognition by the rest of the family.

It is possible to guard against this by at least recognizing the truth of your relationship as it stands. You may not be able to do more for now; sometimes just leaving the business unfinished can be the best way of resolving it. Later, when the worst of grief is over and you feel stronger, you may be able to look at the relationship again.

Role Reversal

One of the most painful experiences while a parent is dying is dealing with her loss of strength and capabilities. Coming to terms with the way illness has invaded your mother's privacy and the way she has become weak is difficult. Both of you may have trouble adapting to role reversal, with you as the caretaker.

It is extremely easy to fall into self-pity at some point as your parent slips away.

In fact, role reversal occurs in the normal course of events: As your parents grow older, you often have to take care of them more. This reversal is faster and more noticeable if your parent is dying of a terminal illness. Within months or even weeks, your duties may change from helping your walking father out of the car to feeding a bed-ridden invalid with a spoon.

Role reversal can be especially difficult to accept if it interrupts your emotional dependence on either of your parents.

Although Maria and Anita were both in their midtwenties when they lost their mothers, Anita felt far more vulnerable. She felt that she was an immature twenty-five and that her mother was being taken from her at a key point in her life. She had just returned from a year's traveling in Australia and India and she needed her mother to talk with because it was time to make some mature choices in life.

As an experienced nursery-school teacher, Maria at twenty-five was more established. She was also engaged. When the two girls met and developed a kind of friendship at the hospital, Anita felt bitter that Maria had a fiancé to support her through her mother's loss while to all intents and purposes she was alone.

It is extremely easy to fall into self-pity at some point as your parent slips away. Even if you don't feel like a child inside, you may feel that your parent is too young to die. With today's longer life expectancy, death at sixty or even seventy can seem like it's cheating you. Michael, whose father died at seventy-two, certainly felt his dad could have enjoyed a few more years.

Other Relationship Changes

The other great change that takes place is with your living parent, who is likely to be more unhappy than you have ever seen her. Because of this, you can expect unfair anger from her. You may be the recipient of emotional scenes or many silences, both of which are distressing and draining. Feeling powerless is a difficult adjustment, but you may not be able to comfort your other parent as you would like. She may express appreciation of your presence and efforts one day, only to appear cold or angry the next.

Just as with your dying parent, you have to learn to let go of someone who may become harder to reach. Also, you can expect more

> *Just as with your dying parent, you have to learn to let go of someone who may become harder to reach.*

role reversal—for example, taking care of someone who does not care whether he is taken care of. Chapter 8 explores the subject of you and your surviving parent in more detail.

For a start, the best thing to do is forget family roles as much as possible and look at your family as individuals struggling against the same blow.

With such a major event at the center of your life, it will be surprising if your other relationships don't change. Friends, coworkers and neighbors can all seem remote or insensitive. During impending loss and after your parent's death are times when you are likely to feel completely cut off from the mainstream of life. This is especially true if you are deeply involved with your family.

Unfortunately, you may experience a genuine lack of empathy from friends and coworkers. Losing a parent is such a

> *Friends, coworkers and neighbors can all seem remote or insensitive.*

common life event that, while people may express initial sympathy, they may quickly forget your feelings as time goes by.

Few want to hear or talk about death. It is much easier if you can accept this, turning to genuine friends or grief groups for support. This won't last forever. The friends you feel you can't talk to may still be valuable in the future, even if you have to put the friendship on hold for now.

It can also be helpful not to burden the close people in your life with too much responsibility for you during this time. This is partly because friendships change: Closeness comes and goes, according to circumstances. Someone you could pour your heart out to may be invaluable now, and a treasured friend for life, but not someone you'll feel the same need to talk to a year or so from now.

> *Your emotions during this period, although perhaps all-consuming, are not going to be typical for the rest of your life.*

Your emotions during this period, although perhaps all-consuming, are not going to be typical for the rest of your life. If you have a family of your own, or a long-term partner, they can provide welcome support, often just by being there for you.

> ᜒMichael's wife, Joan, knew there was little she could do to help him while his father was dying, but she also knew that it would have been much harder for him to go through it alone. Joan's role varied from receiving 3 A.M. phone calls from Michael in the hospital to calling to cheer up the family with the news that she had gotten her driver's license!
>
> Heather's boyfriend, Will, would often cook a meal for Heather and her mother, Barbara, when they came back from their nightly hospital visits. He also insisted on taking Heather away for the weekend a few times.

Sharing Care—Relationships with Siblings

Family funerals are notorious for disputes, but trouble can be brewing long before that point. Another feature of a parent's death is the way it traps you within the family, causing a return to childhood, especially if you have been living on your own. No matter the circumstances or how old you are, it is difficult to avoid some childhood habits or feelings when you go home. With the established balance of the family upset by the coming death of a father or mother, everyone feels insecure and unsure of his or her role.

> Guy didn't know just what he was supposed to do in the short time he was around his dying father. "Looking back, I think we were all too young to deal with it—neither my two sisters (nineteen and twenty-three at the time) nor myself had any idea what to do. We just brought flowers and kept quiet."

Michael's family had to visit his father, Tom, in two separate groups because of the quarrel that had divided the family years earlier. Michael was deeply upset that the family was arguing above his father's deathbed.

> "I felt Dad was crying out for love. What really caused me the deepest pain was the fact that one of my brothers didn't seem to care. He'd be reading the paper over Dad's head or looking at his watch."

It's true that some people are better at deathbeds than others, yet this is a time when such petty differences can be a problem. This tense situation brings out the worst in each family member.

Even without big complications, it is common to feel that you are doing more than other family members who are insensitive and neglecting the dying parent. You may feel that your motives are better than theirs in regard to giving your time and attention. This kind of jealous fighting for the dying parent's attention is natural; to feel special to the dying parent is a profound need.

To feel special to the dying parent is a profound need.

> Anita used to feel she was the only one who brought the right kind of flowers to her mother in the hospital, although she recognized this as an emotional rather than a rational observation. She felt she was justified for being angry at her brother,

Louis, for constantly sitting at her mother's bedside
and trying to cheer her up with jokes and chatter
that Anita felt were both inappropriate and tiring for
her mother.

One child is often the "coper" of the family, usually the eldest.
This is the one who shops, cooks and makes sure that mom or dad
takes the right medicine.

༄ The oldest of the three children, Anita, who
returned home for a while, easily fell into the role
but increasingly realized she would have to share
this status with her sister, Karen.

Both women felt this would be much easier
without the well-meaning interference of their
brother. Once he was forced by business pressure to
return to his home in another city, Anita and Karen
established a much easier balance, taking turns
sharing their mother's care until her death.

Having something to do helps break down the frustration of
this period. Perhaps you can work out a duties list with the rest of
the family. Having a definite list of things to do, such as watching
your parents' house, stopping the newspaper delivery, watering the
plants or walking the dog can help distract
you and your family and give you all a
sense of importance and control.

*Having something to
do helps break down
the frustration of
this period.*

Sharing duties avoids one person
trying to take everything on his or her
shoulders. If there have been family feuds,
you could agree to a temporary truce, to work together to deal
with the most important thing: your parent's death.

You might find it helpful to see your family socially, especially
if you don't normally. Perhaps close friends or husbands and wives
could be asked to step in and provide some emotional coolness if
tempers become heated. Otherwise, hard as it might be, it can be
more helpful to detach yourself emotionally from the family circle
and just let others be the way they are.

This is certainly one of the most unstable times a family can go through. Decisions have to be made, new emotions have to be dealt with and relationships with brothers and sisters you may not have seen for a while must be tested during this trying time.

Using the Time Left

A parent's death may appear to be made up of little problems and major heartache. At this time it is helpful to step back from the pressures of everyday life and the coming death to take an objective look at the situation.

> *Dying people can lead full lives, using the time to travel, start new hobbies or fulfill lifelong ambitions.*

No one wants to feel her mother's life has no further value once the prognosis has been given. Even if your mother is weary of life and even if death comes as a relief, this final illness does not make her nonexistent.

Dying people can lead full lives, using the time to travel, start new hobbies or fulfill lifelong ambitions. Even when major activity is no longer possible, your parent is still living.

> ♉ Heather brought soft clay into the hospital for her father to model tiny animals when he was strong enough, and she would take them home to bake and paint herself.
>
> While he was still at home, Michael's father appreciated the roast chicken and fruit cookies Michael's wife sent over.
>
> Maria would go out and get her mother some ice cream or a new book to read. Maria's mother also liked to have her daughter help with her make-up before the doctor's visit, saying that it would be the doctor who died of fright if he saw her without it!

To be labeled *dying* is a major blow to a person's identity, so it can also be helpful to your parent if you allow her to give to you, as you give to her. This was one of the things Anita came to realize in her relationship with her mother.

❧ "She needed to know that she was still useful to me, that she still mattered. She wanted to make sure I would choose the right career and the right man even though she often became angry and we never were able to discuss things properly. I know part of her fussing was that she hated losing control, dying when we both felt I still needed her."

Anita's mother wanted to give advice but didn't quite know how or in what form to give it. Anita understood that this was her way of showing that she cared.

> *Taken day by day, life can still yield meaning, richness and peace, even in small doses.*

Because we tend to think in terms of what *we* can do for the dying, we can forget the need for dying parents to give care to those around them. Parents want to leave their children well-provided for emotionally. It is, after all, in a parent's nature to be concerned for his children, even after they become adults.

Also, someone who is given a short time to live may live a few more years and may intend to make the most of those years before she becomes bedridden. This was the case with Maria's mother.

❧ Maria's mother, Susan, who had always been an energetic soul, had several remissions in what was diagnosed as terminal cancer. When she was well, she was as much her old self as possible, going out, visiting people, handing out birthday and Christmas cards, and deaf to all suggestions that she should rest or take it a bit easier.

Maria, at first resentful of the way her mother gave of herself, was later able to see this as the need of a dying person to give.

This may be a time when giving and caring on both sides can be appreciated in its purest form, without being clouded by the usual distractions of work, money and so on.

The curtailing of time is one of the hardest things to accept about this period; life has suddenly shrunk to a few months, a few weeks, and it may be necessary to define living in terms of *being* rather than *doing*.

Just to have your parent be himself or herself—bossy, humorous, cranky, opinionated—can be immensely reassuring. Taken day by day, life can still yield meaning, richness and peace, even in small doses.

Initiating the Grieving Process

Your future well-being depends on releasing your grief—it must come out. While there is life, there may be hope, which means you can sometimes put off grieving. But, there are all sorts of little griefs before the day of the death.

Grief may come when your parent becomes too weak to travel or fluff a pillow. She may also lose interest in matters that used to concern her, such as her children and their families.

The suspense of this pre-death period can often cause a kind of numbness. You may continue to live as best you can, without letting too many emotions slow you, perhaps waiting for the right moment to let go and start feeling your grief.

Perhaps you feel that the right moment isn't until *after* death, that you'll let it all out then. For now, you may feel that you need to stay numb in order to cope. But, it is worth noting that the grieving process can and does start before death.

Don't force yourself to grieve. Grief is not something you "let out" to feel healthy again. It isn't a case of saying that the sooner you begin to grieve, the sooner it will be over and everything will be better. Grief is not a condition that you get over like an illness. It is a life experience that demands a long-term response and

Grief is not something you "let out" to feel healthy again.

cannot be rushed through or swept away. Grief can be positive: There is no substitute for an experience that brings new skills and new strengths you can use for the rest of your life.

It may be possible to grieve before your parent dies, especially if she is ill for months or even years. Grief stops and starts for a long time before it is really absorbed. By the time you feel you can resume your life without a huge burden of sorrow, you will have become a different person. You will be someone who has changed deeply from the grief you have lived through.

Losing a parent is a time when you need your closest relationships, your friends and relatives, to provide support in a way you never thought of before. You need to find a balance between taking care of yourself, looking after others, and finding some kind of outside support.

Emotions are likely to be rough and raw instead of the gentle deathbed scenes you may have pictured. To get through this period more easily, you may need to suspend judgment, especially where friendships are concerned.

Last, you can help yourself by holding on to the knowledge that your essential identity has not changed, even if you feel confused or lost in the upheaval caused by your mother's or father's death.

3

When Death Comes

NO MATTER WHAT EMOTIONAL PREPARATIONS we have made for death, it is hard to accept when it actually does take place—our sense of reality is shaken so deeply. It's surprising how much we need our day-to-day routine to feel strong.

Even small changes in life can be upsetting, such as having your desk moved at work or having a toothache. Now, with the normal routine destroyed, with the unthinkable actually happening, your mind may be unable to believe or understand what is going on. The time up to death, the event itself and the time just afterward touch us too closely to be viewed within the normal parameters of life.

Like it or not, we are cut off from the events of an ordinary day. Like war, death cuts through all ordinary conditions, but rest assured that you will eventually assimilate this experience into the fabric of your life. Things will return to normal; new beginnings will emerge.

Things will return to normal; new beginnings will emerge.

You will discover unsuspected sources of strength and maturity within yourself, but the process will be painful. You will forge new bonds with other people—not immediately when you feel that no one can understand or enter into your grief, but in the long term.

There's a temptation after dealing with a parent's death to divide people into insiders (those who have also suffered) and outsiders (those still living in ignorance of what death really means). When this mellows with time, it can leave you with a valuable appreciation of other people and their problems.

Finally, you may feel stronger for having had to confront some of life's deepest questions, for having looked death in the face and perhaps formulated your own concept of it to sustain you through life.

All this is in the future, outside the immediate context of your parent dying, but hang on to the idea. There is indeed a future, more varied and enriching than you can imagine in the desolate circumstances of the present.

Last Visits: Waiting for Death

Few things are more distressing than the weeks and days just before death, when you don't know exactly when death will take place. Wondering, as you climb the hospital steps, how your father will be today, how much further he may have slipped away and whether he will die while you're there can leave you in a constant state of stress. And if he does die, how on earth will you be able to bear it?

It's a time of great confusion, when a day can feel like a week, and a week like a year. If death is slow, you may find a time when your emotions turn off. After expecting yet another night to be the last, attending your father's deathbed becomes a matter of sheer physical endurance.

> ≈ The doctors told Michael that his father was dying, but it was about three weeks before this actually happened. During most of this time, his father, Tom, was unconscious, his wasted body looking dead already. The family couldn't understand how Michael kept going to the hospital.
>
> Michael, who expected every day to be the last, wanted to spend as much time with his dad as possible, especially because he knew Tom hadn't wanted to be alone while conscious.
>
> But with this grueling visiting routine, which meant staying into the early hours every day, Michael became absolutely exhausted. His own family suffered, too—his wife would wait up for him, or for his phone calls from the hospital, expecting every call to deliver the news.

The Dying Person's Need to Grieve

Anita's mother slipped into a coma during her last week of life, but Anita was horrified to notice her weeping in her sleep, "crying for her life," as a nurse put it.

The dying person *does* need to cry for his life—to mourn the mistakes, the missed opportunities and the less-than-perfect relationships. Above

> *Like all mourning, the grief of the dying is a private process.*

all, he needs to mourn the simple fact that time is running out and there will be no further chances to do more or make things right.

Going through this grief can help a dying person come to terms with the unsatisfactory elements in his life. So, although bitterly upsetting to see, look at it as a painful route toward peace.

Like all mourning, the grief of the dying is a private process. This is partly what makes it so painful to see: the stony face, the numbed self-absorption in your father as he shuts you out. Sometimes there is little you can do but let him go through it.

You can help share the pain, but it can seem as if this sharing does not get through to your father. Nevertheless, the very ill often want company even if they aren't up to talking. You can help just by being there.

You may also be able to help in other ways, especially if your father gives you an opening and starts to talk about his feelings. This is no longer a question of talking about the fact that he is dying, or of asking if there is anything he wants done after death. It's a time to check on any private fears he may have and to acknowledge your father's feelings of grief at losing his life.

These conversations can be very simple. If your father says he's depressed, all you can really say is "I'm very sorry to hear that." Because once you've spoken the truth, what more is there to say? You cannot console him with easy comments to the effect that he'll be better soon.

But you don't need to make the situation more painful with too many raw emotions or by pushing him to talk further. By now you may feel you've been through all the possible emotions anyway and are squeezed dry.

It may be almost as much of an effort for you to talk as for your father to talk. Try to follow where he leads. He may simply want you to be around. Being shut up alone with his grief can be just as isolating for your dying father as it is for you.

Even if your parent is in a coma, like Anita's mother, she may still be aware to some degree of what is going on around her. It is quite common for a previously comatose person to wake up suddenly and be able to repeat conversations that have been going on around her bedside.

Holding your parent's hand and giving simple words of reassurance and love is not a waste of energy. As death comes closer, hearing is the last sense to go.

Letting Go

There comes a moment when our parent needs to die, and we need to let go. But what is *letting go,* exactly? By no means is it a decision not to think about your parent anymore, to become indifferent or turn off emotionally. One way to define it is as a deep acceptance of our lack of power in the face of death.

> *There comes a moment when our parent needs to die, and we need to let go.*

This is something we all know we should have, but having to deal with it is just about impossible unless death forces itself on us. Who wants to let go of their mother behind the drawn curtains of a bed in a public ward? Who feels they can let go after a 2 A.M. phone call from the nurse saying their father has finally died?

> ℀ Anita could not accept her mother's final submission. It seemed so strange in someone who had always been a fighting spirit. It took Anita a long time to accept that her mother may have made important inner changes during her last week or so in a coma.

It is worth noting that Anita's trouble with letting go was compounded by the troubles she had always had in her relationship with her mother. At a fundamental level, it just didn't seem right that her mom was no longer there to fight with.

There's a fine line between caring for your dying parent, an activity that belongs to life, and accepting his gradual departure. The death process itself often helps—as the dying person becomes more remote, it becomes easier to let go. But there's still plenty of room for the denial that is such a big part of grief.

Being Present at Death

Witnessing death is usually worse in anticipation than in reality. Even if the time until death is distressing, death itself is often a peaceful moment, as Heather found out.

> ⊃ℂ "It was all very calm—after all, we knew it was going to happen. We'd been prepared for it for months, now. It was like something that just had to be. And it was nice because we were all there."

It's the terrible days and hours beforehand that can be so traumatic, with your father wired to machines in intensive care or in a geriatric ward. He's become almost unrecognizable due to illness. The medical treatment may make you feel your parent has lost the right to die with dignity.

In the last few hours, you will probably see noticeable physical changes. His face may seem to fall in, becoming more skeletal. Breathing becomes irregular and hoarser. He may be given a drug to dry up throat secretions that, although painless to the patient, are distressing to listen to. Often the last breath is especially deep, a kind of long sigh before life departs. That is the physical sum of it.

Witnessing death is usually worse in anticipation than in reality.

But, as one hospital chaplain pointed out, people have a habit of dying much as they lived. They may keep a family dancing by the bedside like the family danced around them in life. They may hang on for days and days and then finally die when everyone's out of the room. They may be quiet and unobtrusive, as if they didn't want to be a bother.

Many people value being present at their parent's death.

Many people value being present at their parent's death. This doesn't mean it suits everyone, but actually seeing your father dead can take away some of that childish horror of the unknown that haunts our adult minds.

A dead body has been described by many people as essentially a vehicle, something no longer inhabited. There is even a poem that compares the body to a car that has been parked, engine off and lights out, while the driver has walked off down the road to home.

In some cases, you might want to do more than merely look at the dead body. Michael combed his father's hair for him. Anita put her mother's engagement ring on her finger because her father wanted her to be buried with it.

One woman, a nurse, helped to prepare her mother for burial as a last act of love. Another nurse who lost her mother refused when asked if she would like to do the same. It is up to you how much you choose to do.

Losing Both Parents

If both your parents die, either simultaneously or within a few months of each other, you experience a more drastic change of identity than with the loss of just one parent. Having your parents alive is a sort of backup you hardly know you have until it's taken away. One particular effect of this is not being sure where your home is now, as Stephen found.

> "Before my parents died, I would always call Canada home. I'd say, 'I'm going home for Christmas, I'm going home to see my parents,' even though I'd been living in the United States for fifteen years."

Stephen didn't own his own home and he had no children, but even someone with a family of his own may feel he has lost his home. A concentration of your family in a certain area may become more important to you.

On the other hand, you may feel that the time has come for a new start, especially if family relations have been strained. You might uncover some great relatives who become lifelong friends as a result! The quest for your roots can lead to journeys of all kinds, sometimes wonderful, sometimes uncomfortable, sometimes even embarrassing.

> Jackie, who lost both parents, sought out aunts and uncles she hadn't seen for many years. After several awkward visits, she realized their lives were barely connected to hers. Nonetheless, she moved to St. Louis, her mother's hometown and the scene of many childhood vacations.
>
> But she felt little sense of homecoming and became ill and depressed, haunted by memories of the past that had no real place in her present life. After a year, Jackie moved back to Indiana with a great sense of a relief. She never visited Missouri again.

This touches on an important point: If you feel driven to find roots or family connections, you may go through some unpleasant experiences. But the simple act of going through the process can leave you more open to choose your own environment for the rest of your life.

The way you lose both parents is important. If they both die in an accident or disaster, your reactions will be different than

The way you lose both parents is important.

if four or five years separate both deaths, which can happen during long-lasting diseases. (See chapter 4 for more on how to deal with sudden death.) Another possibility is that they both die of an illness within a short time of each other—a tragic push into adult life that is not that common but does happen.

> Clare, in her early twenties, nursed both her parents through cancer and saw them die within weeks of each other. The worst time for her was immediately after death. During their illnesses she was sustained by her active, caring role. But she went through a difficult time when she found herself an orphan at twenty-six.

The phenomenon of the old couple who die within months of each other is not uncommon. The death of one partner after thirty or forty years of marriage is a profound interruption of life systems that is more traumatic than many elderly people can take. The same thing can happen at a slightly younger age, too.

> ❧ Jackie was never quite sure why her mother died a few months after her father. He had died of cancer in his seventies, and her mother, as Jackie put it, "just seemed to curl up and die, too. I honestly think she died of grief, of not knowing what to do with herself once my father had gone."

Incidentally, this is a reaction that many people fear from even younger parents, especially if their bereaved father or mother expresses feelings of not being able to go on without the other. On the positive side, it is amazing how resilient the separated halves of the most devoted partnerships can be. It isn't always the people you expect who die of heartbreak.

Just Afterward

No matter what emotional preparations we may have made for impending death, it is hard to deal with when it actually happens. This tends to mark the real beginning of questioning the nature of death.

No matter what emotional preparations we may have made for impending death, it is hard to deal with when it actually happens.

Where has the person gone? You may not even consider something as complex as the soul, but instead something simpler. It is difficult to think about something so abstract, but you may wonder about details.

What has become of all the little habits, such as a certain way of knotting a tie, always humming the same song or constantly leaving the utensil drawer open? It is too much for the human mind to cope with. In the immediate aftermath of death, you may ask further questions. You may try to see where your parent has gone, trying to follow as far as you can go. This is partly why you feel so isolated in immediate grief.

This is a time when the least little word can set off pain. Many people have reported how tender and bruised they felt in the first few weeks after the death.

> ⚶ For Guy, every little word grated on his nerves. He couldn't stand listening to the news in case there was any mention of hospitals or death, and he couldn't drive past the hospital where his father had died. These feelings faded gradually over the next eighteen months.

You may feel that the emotions you are experiencing are not appropriate. Pain and tears may not come, you may not feel sorrow, but the strain of death may cause extreme fatigue.

The period just after a death can be a time of great relief, a time to let all the exhaustion out, especially if you have been involved in a lengthy dying process.

Michael's nightly visits to the hospital really caught up with him after his father finally died. Maria realized how much her stamina had been depleted in her mother's last days.

> ⚶ "It sounds awful, but I just stayed in bed the day after Mom died and got my sister to bring me breakfast. I felt so shattered, as if I'd been hit over the head with a club, drained in every way. I wanted someone to take care of me for a change. I felt I'd been giving out so much, I just couldn't make any more effort at all."

This feeling of extreme fatigue may last for several weeks. Remember, this is a time when you need to take care of yourself. If you are staying with or live close to your family, perhaps you could take turns taking care of each other for a while.

Or it might be a good idea to stay with a close friend who will feed you a hot meal and provide a comfortable place for you to sit and contemplate what has happened. This is probably a friend who doesn't mind accommodating you when you want to be alone.

Of course, you have responsibilities of your own and may have to struggle with a tiring job or caring for your children. But within the context of these duties, taking care of yourself must be a priority.

The Impact on Your Own Family

If you have a family of your own, comfort can be easier to come by, although this period immediately after death can be an unexpected strain. If your partner has been through it all with you, he or she may feel less sorrow and more relief at the death of someone who was not a natural parent. Your partner may want to get on with normal living.

> Michael's wife, Joan, felt that her abilities as a caretaker had been overused during his father's illness. She was also fed up with his quarreling family and wanted Michael to herself again. But he would stay in bed late whenever possible and sleep a lot during the afternoons and on weekends.
>
> While Joan understood his exhaustion in one way, in another she was annoyed at how Michael's father, who had never paid much attention to her, continued to play an influential part in their lives. The situation was worsened by the demands of their children, which Michael couldn't always help with.

In other words, families have to be ready to extend their support after death *throughout* the period of grief. It is natural to feel a little jealousy, but it is unrealistic to make normal demands on someone who is stunned and isolated by the impact of death.

Losing a parent can separate the closest couples for a while. The grieving partner may feel impatience with his partner who doesn't understand. It is hard for two people to see things exactly alike when one has lost a parent and the other has not, although some people mourn an in-law's death as if he were their own flesh and blood. This is a time for the nongrieving partner to take the lead, to assume more responsibilities until the spouse has regained the balance lost in his or her immediate grief.

4

Sudden Death

ALTHOUGH MANY PEOPLE LOSE THEIR PARENTS relatively late in life to lingering illnesses, some lose their parents without warning. This may be due to a short illness, or a sudden collapse, with death following minutes or hours later. Sadly, this is not uncommon in any country where heart disease is a leading cause of death.

Many illnesses can cause a speedy death, such as heart attack, a stroke, pneumonia or even a rapidly developing cancer. While we know accidents are always possible, it is still a tremendous shock when one causes death. Murders and suicides are less common but also traumatic and sudden.

The impact of sudden death is different from the impact of a lingering one, especially at first. Life changes drastically from one minute to the next. There's no time to prepare, although sometimes heart attacks or other illnesses follow warning signs.

It's hard to appreciate the shock unless you've been through it. You need time to absorb the news and cope with the physical sensations of shock. You may have to cancel plans and expectations and even alter your view of the world.

You may have to cancel plans and expectations and even alter your view of the world.

You will never feel the same again about a life in which such things can happen, in which the impossible has become fact and still can't be understood. This is when we catch on to the difference between knowing that such events do take place and having one of them strike our own lives.

This difference produces a large gap between the way we experience life before and the way we experience it after.

Eventually, the event becomes part of the pattern of our lives. It becomes a reference point, a time from which we may feel that our present identities have developed. One of the main aspects of any parent's death is the way it forms a before-and-after scenario, with different views and identities belonging to each time period. The divide is that much sharper with sudden death.

We tend to have a mental picture of our parents living comfortably in retirement and fading away peacefully at the end of busy, useful lives. When this is cut short by sudden or violent death, grief is that much more difficult to work through. It's more difficult for both you *and* your surviving parent, who may need more of your support than if the death had been gradual and expected.

In addition to the fact that the shock is worse, mourning may be more complicated and longer. You may have more work to do during the initial grief period. Often, finding some comforting meaning in what has happened is more difficult.

It is also common to idealize a person who has died suddenly or violently.

You may be tempted to blame your dead father or mother for the way in which they died. It is also common to idealize a person who has died suddenly or violently.

When you hear the news of sudden death, you can understand the expression "it's a blow." News of this kind is a physical blow—you may feel as if you've been hit in the body, the air knocked out of you. To be told that your mother is dying is bad enough (as discussed in chapter 1), but it's true that while there is life, there is hope—it isn't the same as being told that she is actually dead.

Shock can last several days after sudden death and its effects must not be underestimated. Again, take care of yourself by keeping warm and drinking plenty of (nonalcoholic and noncaffeinated) fluids, even if you can't eat.

You may feel numb, suspended from normal life, a reaction that can actually be protective. It can give you time to let the news sink in before you start experiencing any of the feelings connected with the situation.

Once you do start feeling, the anger may be greater than if your parent had died gradually. A prolonged dying period can make dealing with anger easier because you have more time to adjust, although a sudden death may provide you with a focus for your anger. For example, if your parent died in a car crash, you may direct your anger at the other driver or drivers involved.

This is especially true following large-scale disasters, such as Hurricane Irene, which recently struck the southeastern United States in 1999, or the Flood of '93, which hit the midwestern United States. Research suggests that it can actually be helpful if relatives of those killed are able to direct their anger toward other things. These *Sudden death is more often heard of than witnessed.* things can range from pressing charges against those responsible or campaigning for better safety precautions.

Sudden death is more often heard of than witnessed. Because of this, you may feel anguish, wondering what your father's or mother's last moments were like, whether they were terrifying or painful.

It is natural for their seconds or minutes of dying to become your hours of emotional distress. Turning off your thoughts by sheer willpower alone is not easy and often impossible. At some point, you may need to talk to someone (see Interrupted Relationships later in this chapter and chapter 9).

The fact that you weren't there when he died can also be a source of long-lasting regret. The fact that *no one* may have been there can also be stressful. You may have to deal with the lengthy, painful mental process of second-guessing: *If only* your father had taken a later train, *if only* your mother had consulted a doctor earlier and so on. Sudden deaths are often bizarre, like nightmares, because they are so unexpected. This is especially true when they are accidents.

- Peter's father died hours after a baseball hit him on the bridge of the nose.
- Glen's father died a few days after being crushed in a crowd on New Year's Eve.
- Ruth's mother died after being hit by a large garbage container that a truck was unloading.

Adapting the strangeness of some events to the everyday world in which you have lived so far is a daunting experience that may also present religious challenges. It's probably more accurate to say that adaptation of this kind isn't really possible. Sudden death, more than any other kind of death, may force us to re-examine our values and the way we live our lives.

Sudden Illness

Many people know someone who's died of a stroke or heart attack. Strokes and heart attacks don't always come without warning, such as a period of poor health, some ominous symptoms or even a previous attack. Even so, the death itself is often sudden.

> ⅔ Colin knew his father, Joe, had endured at least one heart attack years ago. His father's health had been poor ever since. But when Joe died at seventy-nine of another heart attack, it was still a shock because the death itself was so sudden: Colin's mother found Joe sitting dead in front of the television one afternoon.

In this kind of situation, you may feel helpless anger at your parent if you think he somehow could have avoided the death. This is not always related to the facts. Colin certainly felt that Joe was to blame for not taking care of himself better, although Joe had changed his lifestyle a lot after his first illness.

You may also feel like your parent was cut down in her prime, especially if a heart attack causes death at an early age, as often happens. The lack of dignity that precedes death from a heart attack or stroke can be especially disturbing.

It is distressing to live with the mental image of your mother falling to the pavement and being unable to get up or finding your father half-dressed and dead. You need to work through the sadness and

> *In the long term, don't allow the image of death to color your view of your parent's entire life.*

awkwardness of this kind of death as you grieve. In the long term, don't allow the image of death to color your view of your parent's entire life.

If your father or mother dies after a short illness, you are likely to go through similar shock, but, sadly, this will be preceded by a few terrible days. We are so accustomed to the rescues performed by modern medicine that we're not prepared for it to fail.

> ᴈℂ Doreen's elderly mother, who had a weak heart, was admitted to intensive care with severe gastroenteritis. Despite the best efforts of the staff, she died three days later.

In this case, the urge to blame the medical staff can be even stronger than with a terminal illness, although Doreen had nothing but praise for the efforts of her local hospital. You may also feel that you could have stepped in with preventive measures earlier. Doreen says:

> ᴈℂ "I thought I could have done something, like visiting her a day or two earlier and making her a cup of coffee because she got dehydrated. I was really upset with her for not picking up the phone and telling me she didn't feel well until it was too late. I guess she didn't want to be a bother. She was always like that."

Any illness in a parent can seem like a reproach. You may think it happened because you weren't watching out for them. You want a chance to make it right when they're well again.

When death defies your expectations, it may take a long time and a lot of reassurance before this guilt subsides. Talk to the medical professionals who attended your parent because you need to know they did everything possible.

You could also ask other family members and friends to give a more objective appraisal of how much you did for your parent. This can help to remind you that you can only do so much.

Accident

Some people feel that an accident is at least a quick way to go. Others would prefer to know they are dying to better prepare for the end. It can be consoling if your father or mother died at once or soon after an accident, enduring just a short time of pain, if any at all.

What isn't easy to overcome is the strength of your own mental and emotional denial. Ruth, a thirty-eight-year-old nurse, was called home from work one afternoon with the news that her mother was dead.

> ⁀ "That night, I kept thinking I had to call and tell her the news. I just couldn't believe that she wouldn't be there. I always went to her with anything important. This happened again and again during the night—I was dozing on and off, I couldn't sleep, and I kept thinking that I had to call my mother, that there was something important to tell her.
> "Every so often I'd wake up and realize that this was a true-life nightmare, that if you believe in hell, this was it. I had no sense of time—I thought I would never come out of this, that this was the end for me, too."

This mental work is extraordinarily exhausting. Out of habit, your mind searches for some relief or distraction so it doesn't keep coming back to the terrible news. The shock doesn't come once, but hundreds of times. You may also need to replay the details of the accident in your mind again and again, not just at first, but for months to come. A growing anger can be especially evident after an accident. The apparent senselessness of it, the fact that it might have been avoided, can easily make you want to blame someone or something.

✠ Ruth couldn't forgive the truck driver who'd
unloaded the garbage container that killed her
mother. Although the driver was overwhelmed with
distress himself, Ruth thought he was no better than
a murderer. She couldn't bring herself to believe that
it was just an accident, feeling that there must have
been some intention, some conscious act.

You may be tempted to blame your parent, just as with a heart
attack or other illness. It is common to feel that with a little more
care the accident could have been
avoided. You may think your parent
was foolishly courting death by, say,
riding a bike on busy roads, or, in
Ruth's mother's case, waiting to cross
the street right by the garbage truck.

> *You may be tempted to blame your parent, just as with a heart attack or other illness.*

This blame is usually unfounded, although sometimes there is
a link between a person's lifestyle and the possibility of death. For
example, one woman's mother, a heavy drinker, fell down the
stairs drunk and broke her neck. Generally, though, this "if only"
type of thinking has a limited relation to the reality of the event.
Accepting the accident as it happened requires a great deal of
work. Because accidents threaten everybody's safety, the need to
find someone to blame is that much stronger.

Murder

Susan's father died in a stabbing incident on a busy street—one of
those senseless, one-in-a-million chances. For months afterward
she repeatedly imagined what happened in several different ways.

✠ "I felt so completely miserable that he'd died in
that way—alone—that there hadn't been anyone
there to help him."

The solitude of murder is hard to bear and so are the awful
circumstances. The father or mother you once looked up to is a
victim of a vicious and unreasonable act, an act that can't be
undone. The murder of a parent can be particularly frightening if

it triggers any childhood memories of wanting to kill your father or mother. What angry child doesn't at some point threaten a parent with death, either aloud or in silence?

Sudden death, such as accidents and murders in particular, can make you wonder: How could they have let it happen to them? How could the parent I knew have allowed such a thing?

You may decide that if this could happen, you really didn't know your parent at all, that he had some secret up his sleeve that was only revealed by his death. Behind this lurks the old idea that the way we live determines our death, that at some level we all consent to our death or even choose it.

> ⊱ Susan was torn apart by her suspicions about her murdered father, since the murderer was never caught and no motive was established for the crime. Had there been some side of his life that the family didn't know about? Had he been pursuing some secret life that led to his own destruction?
>
> "The police asked us if we knew of anyone who had a grudge against him. The idea was so foreign to be attributed to Dad, just so unlike the person we knew. He was the last person to get himself murdered, he was a civilized man. Was there something we didn't know about him? I've just had to live with that mystery."

The idea that the victim on some unknown level consented to his death—that there are oppressors and victims—can be traced back to primitive societies. The idea of *karma* (the person meeting the experiences he needs in order to grow spiritually) also plays a part in such thinking, perhaps a rather guilt-ridden part.

Some people are aware that their time has come.

Under the influence of this century's psychological pioneers, such as Freud and Jung, we are also accustomed to thinking of ourselves as having unconscious minds with unconscious purposes. These ideas need to be handled carefully so they do not add to the anguish you feel after sudden or violent death. They need to be distinguished from the old lady who quietly waves away food and medicine because she feels it is her time to go. Some people are aware that their time has come.

Again, a blatant disregard for health is another matter. The person who refuses to alter a stressful life and poor diet after a heart attack or the one who refuses to give up alcohol when warned of cirrhosis is, on some level, responsible for his own end. But is it fair, let alone true, to accuse someone of a death wish because his life ended in tragedy?

In addition to the anger and guilt we feel at our parents for abandoning us, the death-wish idea could be linked to our view of our parents as powerful, so powerful that only they could decide on their deaths. Perhaps we need to look at how such a death destroys any lingering childhood notions of a parent's invincibility.

Part of you is unable to believe that they didn't have some say in what happened. In the end, we have to respect our parent's privacy. Our control over the way they live and die is strictly limited.

> *In the end, we have to respect our parent's privacy. Our control over the way they live and die is strictly limited.*

Violent deaths bring a chain of often unforeseen consequences: For example, you may have to deal with the police. Investigations can last several months and, after initial police contact, you may hear nothing for a long time. This wait can be agonizing.

Families who've lost someone to murder speak of the double assault they endure: not just the violent death of a loved one, but the intrusion of police, coroners and other agents of the law. They may not be able to bury or even see the body. Information given can be spotty and irregular, adding to their distress. Eventually there may be a trial to attend, which reopens all the old wounds.

Hatred of the murderer and the burning desire to bring him or her to justice can be extremely powerful. Publicity also adds to the confusion and distress of this time. You should always consider exactly how much and what you choose to say to the press or TV reporters, especially because you may live to regret what you tell them. To cope with the additional pressures, consider a victim support group. You will gain not only support but also tools with which to confront these problems. Life will have more order and purpose, both of which can be important when it comes to living through grief.

Suicide

Suicide brings long-term feelings of sorrow, anger and guilt. Why didn't she come to us with the problem instead of taking this drastic step? Why didn't she visit and be taken care of for a few days? Did she really see us as useless? Couldn't we have been allowed to care for her for a change?

These feelings of rejection, which exist with any death, are even stronger with suicide. Indeed, the antisocial nature of suicide is why it is traditionally regarded as taboo. Only in recent years has suicide ceased to be seen as a criminal act around the world.

> *The guilt and remorse that suicide brings can be devastating.*

Suicide may appear to affect only one person, but it is often seen as violence against others. It may involve others by means of notes to which there can be no reply. The guilt and remorse that suicide brings can be devastating.

But the confused feelings of those who commit suicide cannot be taken as valid statements by those left behind. Psychologists are extremely doubtful as to whether *rational* suicide ever exists, believing that some degree of mental disturbance usually accompanies suicide. But this can be particularly hard to comprehend if, as sometimes happens, the motive for the suicide was apparently unselfish.

> Emily's mother committed suicide after being diagnosed with advanced ovarian cancer. She was unable to face the prospect of being such a burden on her family. Emily was confused by this: Didn't her mother's action seem to blame them? Did she consider the family incapable of going through the

ordeal? Wasn't it patronizing of her to take matters into her own hands? Or was it a death full of dignity and self-sacrifice?

To all such questions, the family of the suicide victim is left to find their own answers if they can. Unfortunately, part of coming to terms with what happened may be accepting that you will never truly know the answers.

One unforeseen problem of both murder and suicide is how to explain the death to others in the future. You may feel it's an unnecessary burden to put up with the shock and curiosity of others who were not involved with the death.

You never have to talk just to satisfy someone else's curiosity.

When someone asks what your mother died of, you can avoid having to explain with a short answer, such as "she died in an accident."

Whether you choose to say more will depend on your own feelings and the nature of the curiosity. You never have to talk just to satisfy someone else's curiosity, be it a friend, counselor, therapist or the press.

Interrupted Relationships

One of the features of sudden death is that it allows no time to wrap up unfinished business. Things you might have said during a terminal illness remain unspoken; the relationship is ended just as it is.

> Glen argued with his father about an unpaid loan and avoided him for a month while he tried to get the money together. His regret that his father hadn't seen him as more responsible was one of the most persistent features of his grief.

If you have established a more mature, equal relationship with your parent, it can be just as much of a blow to be suddenly deprived of it.

❧ Colin had just started getting to know his father after his dad's first heart attack. Since that illness, his father, Joe, formerly an irritable person, had mellowed, becoming milder and more open. He was eager to tell stories of his youth, was more interested in Colin's two children and he generally took more time to sit and talk with people.

You may have to accept that sometimes relationships are incomplete because of limited communication.

At least in terminal illness you have a chance to prepare yourself for the death and to tell your father how you feel about him more completely. Coming to terms with a quick end to a relationship is more complex and takes longer. The mind needs to work through the regrets and loose ends during initial grief, rather than during the time leading up to death.

You may have to accept that sometimes relationships are incomplete because of limited communication. Idealizing a parent who has died suddenly is often the result of a noncommunicative relationship.

❧ Colin was bitterly regretful for all the long talks he and his father would never have. He would even have imaginary conversations in his head. When he mentioned this to his mother, she thought for a moment and then replied, "But you used to just stare at the TV together most of the time!"

Idealizing a relationship or focusing on one aspect of it can be a way to manage your loss. This can give structure to the relationship until you feel strong enough to admit that imperfections did exist. Some feel a need to do something more to create this structure, to mark the ending of a relationship and complete the unfinished business.

❧ Ruth was deeply upset that the sweater she had been knitting for her mother would now remain unfinished. She decided to complete it and give it to her aunt, who had been her mother's favorite sister.

Glen used the money he owed his father to buy a small used car for his mother, to make her life easier.

On the advice of his grief support group, Colin tried to write a letter to his father, found he couldn't and burned his letter. He felt that just *trying* to write the letter got something out of his system.

Must it Control Your Life?

The memories accompanying sudden or violent death are not easy to lose. They may haunt you without mercy in the first months and years of grief. At some point, however, it becomes possible to choose whether you allow these memories to continue to dominate you.

You may reach this point sooner if you talk regularly to someone, such as a grief counselor or a minister. Choose someone (or a few people) who is prepared to listen but whose friendship you won't damage with repeated requests to talk over the death.

Depending on the circumstances of your parent's death, you may be offered help and counseling, especially after a large-scale accident or disaster. Help can be more effective, however, if you choose it. The motivation that comes from within will propel you toward health with more strength than external motivation can offer. Getting to the point of seeking help can be a difficult and lengthy journey.

> *Help can be more effective, however, if you choose it.*

It took Susan two years before she was able to discuss her father's death with anyone. She felt others would turn away from her in repulsion, that their world just couldn't handle such shocking events.

Not being a church-goer, she didn't know where to seek the help she knew she needed badly. She felt isolated during this period. Finally,

she read an article about victim support groups in
the newspaper and, realizing this was what she
wanted, joined one.

In the end, the way your parents died is not a complete
statement about their lives. You have so much more to remember.
To concentrate only on the end deprives not only your parents of
their total identity but you of a broader perspective.

Ask yourself this: How would your parent like to be thought
of? Would he prefer to be thought of as a person who died
dramatically, or as someone who led a reasonably full and useful
life with a fair share of irritation, sacrifice and humor? The answer
to this can help you grieve who your parent was in life, not who
he was in death.

5

Abandoned-Child Grief

READ ANY BOOK ON MOURNING and you will see that reactions to death are well documented, following a defined course of shock, disbelief and so on. Reading the list of expected reactions can make you feel like you are on a conveyor belt of grief, being shuttled along from one emotion to the next.

You may feel that, even though your grief seems isolating, it isn't unique if others can label it so conveniently. But we all react to grief in different ways. Psychological research can provide an idea of the *range* of emotions you may go through, even if you don't actually follow the expected stages.

These kinds of feelings can be heightened by the death of a parent who considered you special, even if you weren't particularly successful in the world. Now that important person is gone and can't recognize your grief. This loss of special identity can make you feel that your grief is ordinary.

The feeling of being an abandoned child gives a different focus to the grief that follows the death of a parent, a reaction that can strike at any age. It is common for people over sixty to see themselves as orphans.

A parent who lives until you are advanced in years can leave you stalled at a certain stage of development. You never have to move ahead from your concept of yourself as someone's child, even if you don't recognize this concept until one of your parents dies.

⊸〔 Colin was fifty-three years old when his father
died of a heart attack. However, Colin felt he could
not do what he wanted most: to grieve as a child.
He felt he needed permission to feel like a child in
an adult society, even to cry out loud.

With his graying hair and aging face, he thought
he was expected to be adult about it all when he
actually felt the paralyzing isolation of a child lost in
a supermarket. Colin was ashamed of the dramatic
terms he needed to describe his emotions.

Coming to terms with your new identity is a major part of
grief. You have to get used to the fact that you are no longer
someone's child. For some people this
always remains impossible.

> *You have to get used to the fact that you are no longer someone's child.*

You may visualize yourself as a
child of a loving parent even after that
parent's death. You believe your parent
remains in your life, looking down from some childlike heaven,
perhaps influencing your life for the better in subtle ways.

In the long term, letting such images fade into the background
constitutes a major part of a new maturity. As much as you love
and depend on a parent, it is also in your nature as a child to want
independence.

The Funeral

The funeral is an important part of grieving. Not only is it a formal
goodbye, it also marks the point from which you first begin to
come to grips with a grief-filled life.

For many, the period between the death and the funeral can
be the worst part of the entire experience, particularly if death
happened quickly without any prolonged wait by your dying
parent's bedside.

⊸〔 Stephen's mother died five hours after going into
the hospital with heart failure. Her death wasn't
entirely unexpected. Her cancer had been controlled
by drugs for the past seven years, but her body was

weakening, including her heart. The few days before
the funeral were absolutely unbearable for Stephen.
Normal life was totally suspended and it was
impossible to do anything except think about
death and try to absorb the loss.

One activity that may ease the painful vacuum of this time
is arranging the funeral. Whatever you do in the arrangements,
funerals (like deaths) tend to mirror the character of the dead
person. Funerals can be gregarious shows or quiet affairs with
few attending, depending on the deceased.

> ᴕ Guy's father's funeral was limited to the
> immediate family and two good friends. Guy had
> always thought his father was well liked, but this
> quiet affair made Guy think his father's life had been
> more limited than he had ever realized. However,
> he sympathized with his mother's desire to respect
> his father's privacy in this way.

> ᴕ Although he was well aware of his father's
> difficult personality, Michael was deeply saddened
> by the fact that no friends attended his father's
> funeral and some family members weren't even
> speaking to each other.
> The entire service seemed to
> underscore just how alienated his
> father had been. Some of his bad-
> tempered ways seemed to affect
> all the details of the events. For
> example, Michael and his oldest brother had an
> argument with the minister before the service about
> exactly when the coffin should be carried in!

Funerals (like deaths) tend to mirror the character of the dead person.

Funeral sermons are often a delicate matter for the person
conducting the service, especially if the departed was not the
easiest person to get along with. To eulogize without offending
grieving family members can take courage! Still, it brings a realistic
warmth to the service if character defects receive their tribute as
well as virtues. This can be as simple as a brief mention.

~{ "Those of us who were privileged to know George, and at times to bear with him," as the minister began. George's daughter, Jane, said the minister described her father perfectly.

"Let's face it, Dad was a bit of a handful sometimes, snapping at the nurses and finding fault with everything you tried to do for him. He was like a big, grumpy child. You loved him, of course, but he did get under your skin! I always saw through him, and the minister did too, and it was nice not to have to pretend he was a saint just because he'd died."

There can be a kind of emptiness, a cold pretense that doesn't fully acknowledge the deceased, complete with his human bundle of imperfections. Sometimes the funeral is a starting point for wondering how much you really did know about your parent's life.

Old friends may turn up whose existence you never suspected, shedding new light on your parent's personality and past. In that regard, old friends who attend the service can be more than just comforting proof of how much your parent was loved.

It can also make you stronger to have parts of your parent's life filled in by people who can tell you about times before your birth.

It can also make you stronger to have parts of your parent's life filled in by people who can tell you about times before your birth. Because you are now the *culture carrier*, as one grief writer put it, you suddenly have a greater need to know your family history.

You need to know more about your new responsibility. You're probably in the process of re-evaluating ideas and attitudes on all kinds of subjects: art, religion, business, education. Measuring your own position compared to the rest of your family can help (see chapter 6).

To talk about someone so dear to you, and to hear him or her spoken about, is a natural desire. This need isn't always recognized by people who are at a loss for words in the face of grief, although this may be less of a barrier with grieving adult children because of the attitude that the death of a parent is somehow less painful because it must be expected. People are less fearful of reminiscing.

People may talk to you instead of your surviving parent to avoid giving him or her pain. You might feel left out at a funeral if most of the sympathy cards are addressed to your surviving parent. This really bothered Stephen, although his mother's funeral was well attended and somewhat comforting.

> *People may talk to you instead of your surviving parent to avoid giving him or her pain.*

〜 "People talked to me, but kind of casually. I felt like a substitute for Dad, like they were talking to me because they didn't dare talk to him, or it wasn't going to be as much of a struggle to talk to me instead of him. And it seemed strange that all the sympathy cards were addressed to him. Only a few came to my brothers and sisters and myself. We were in the background, as though it wasn't really our business."

Any details you can obtain about your lost parent remind you that he was a *person*, not just a father. Other people present a more rounded figure than the one you knew. Part of grief and part of growing up is learning to accept that our parental figures were *individual* adults. As time goes on, a certain lack of knowledge about your dead father is one of the most enduring features of grief. It helps if old friends or family members will talk about him and his life.

Just after the funeral can be a difficult time, especially if your daily routine revolved around your dying father for a while. Suddenly there's no one to visit, no more pajamas to bring home from the hospital to wash and no more wondering if some special drink or food would tempt a fading appetite.

You can pass a flower shop without wondering which type would be best to buy today. If your father has been ill even for a short time, you will probably have built up some kind of routine. It is easy to cling to the tiny details of the routine because they were a last link with your father.

Immediate Mourning

Immediate mourning means roughly the first two years following the death. Later chapters in this book take a look at long-term reactions. While some take two years to live through the worst grief, it can take longer. Chapter 6 looks at factors that delay or complicate mourning.

Your first, most bewildering reaction is difficulty accepting the death of someone close to you. For a few days or longer, you just cannot believe your parent is dead. You keep expecting to see her coming through the door or walking up the front sidewalk.

You keep expecting to see her coming through the door or walking up the front sidewalk.

A parent's death can conjure either fears of separation we had as children or experiences of actual separation, such as being left at a babysitter's, daycare or at school. A child has a deep instinct to cling closely to a parent.

You may have a strong feeling that the dead person is still around. People tell of hearing the voice of the dead person calling for a drink in the middle of the night. Or they go up to their bedroom fully expecting to find them in bed, almost seeing them in the contours of the bedding. Linked to this is a common phenomenon of catching glimpses of the dead person.

> ɔC A few days after her father's death, Heather walked into the sitting room to see him smoking his pipe in his armchair, as usual. The vision vanished after a few seconds.

This is a typical report—seeing the dead person for only a moment. Others tell of feeling someone touch them or brush by them. Heather could actually smell the tobacco her father smoked. You may experience no more than a strong feeling that the person has not yet quite departed. Incidentally, in other cultures, the strong sense of the dead person's presence is explained by the simple fact that the spirit lingers for a few days. Our own psychological jargon calls it *denial*.

Where Have They Gone?

This is the eternal question: What becomes of the personality after death? It's a question that enhances the confusion touched on in chapter 8 as to what becomes of one's characteristics.

> ⚴ After her mother died, Maria would sometimes go into her room and open the closet, which still contained her mother's clothes. She was struck by the faint perfume that lingered even though her mother's body had been cremated weeks before. She just could not reconcile the two facts with each other.

You may feel a childlike need to cry out to your dead parent, to alert her, just as an infant cries out to alert a sleeping parent. Some people cry in their sleep, or wake up to find their father's name on their lips, sometimes years after the death.

Dreaming of the dead person is common. One dream that has been reported a few times is of the dead mother or father trying to make a phone call to their child but having trouble speaking when the receiver is picked up, the voice becoming a squeak or a whisper. Others have told of even more disturbing dreams or nightmares.

> ⚴ Michael would dream of his father and wake up in terror at the force of Tom's anger and rage, which in the dream seemed directed at him. He would also dream of meeting Tom's corpse. The funeral, with Tom's coffin being lowered deep into the ground, had horrified him.

> ⚴ Janie dreamed of a malicious mother who would mock her bitterly until she awoke in tears.

> ⚴ Maria dreamed repeatedly of losing a tiny baby somewhere and of eventually finding it dead, shriveled up or changed into a small, broken wooden doll. At the time, Maria was thinking of starting a family but felt unable to proceed because her mother's death a year before was still hanging over her.

All these dreams persisted for five years after the event, most strongly in the first couple of years and then diminishing gradually.

Sadness

Along with all the other, often complicated reactions to your parent's death, you should expect feelings of bottomless sorrow. Some aren't prepared to feel this painful grief to such a degree or for so long. The sadness sweeps through almost physically, to the exclusion of other emotions. There's sadness for the past, for childhood, for all the memories of the different family homes, vacations and holidays you shared.

Your link with this past is now gone. Shared jokes, nuances of communication with someone you knew longer and better than anyone else (and who knew you), are gone. We feel sad for the parent who is still alive, feeling his or her sorrow as well as our own.

It can be a relief to acknowledge this emotion in all its powerful simplicity. Crying can help you do this.

> ⁂ Michael often found himself in tears for a year after his father's death. His crying sometimes stemmed directly from his train of thought, but sometimes it overwhelmed him unexpectedly. He still cried in the second year, but less frequently.

Crying comes easily to some people, not to others. What can be frightening about crying for a parent is the way your own personality seems to return to childhood. The adult concept of time melts away, and the one person who could comfort you in your grief is not there to do so.

Crying comes easily to some people, not to others.

Sadness merges into self-pity: Who's going to take care of me now? Even if you've been independent for several years, you may not have realized how much you took for granted the fact that your parents were alive, always there if you needed them. Even if you lost only one parent, this center is destroyed, although a new center may develop in time and perhaps within your own family unit, perhaps with one of your brothers or sisters—it could even be you.

Anger

When dealing with anger, accept first that it is a normal part of grief and second that it may cloud your judgment. You may blame the medical profession for your parent's death, the doctors and nurses who cared for her. You may resent other people who still have their parents and are unaware of the loss you have suffered. Above all, this can increase your envious feelings.

> ⁌ Anita's friends just didn't understand and this lack of understanding made them appear insensitive. All around her, friends were visiting their parents on weekends, taking a two-day escape from the all-too-real world. Mothers helped daughters plan their weddings or look at apartments. Part of her knew these friends were only proceeding with their normal lives and the other part was furious at their self-satisfaction and lack of awareness.

Anita had a tendency to be envious, and grief accentuates such characteristics. We may be shaken at how destructive and deep our anger can be, how ragged and messy.

We may be shaken at how destructive and deep our anger can be, how ragged and messy.

> ⁌ In a fit of rage one day Maria tore up all the handmade silk handkerchiefs she'd inherited from her mother. For several years, this episode remained one of her most painful memories of early grief.
>
> Maria continued to be plagued by outbursts of intense rage for many years because she and her mother had experienced such a calm, tranquil death. Maria repressed her anger toward her mother until after her actual death.

It's hard to accept how angry and spiteful we can feel toward a person who seemed to choose to leave us.

It's hard to accept how angry and spiteful we can feel toward a person who seemed to *choose* to leave us. We feel they left us willingly to go on their own personal and private journey. It's easier for most people to express their anger at something or someone else, such as hospital management or a church.

Anger at the dead person exists after any loss and is a natural part of a parent's death. Part of this anger may be related to that sense of exclusion from the adult world you may recall having as a small child. You may remember the anger you felt when a closed door meant your mother or father was too busy to talk to you. Or perhaps they wanted you to go to bed while you wanted to continue whatever activity had your attention at the time. Now that door feels closed forever.

Guilt

To some extent, it is possible to experience survivor guilt after any death, even if the death wasn't part of some disaster. Why should we still be alive when someone else has died? You may also have "if only" feelings to deal with, usually centering around what you believe you should have done but didn't do.

If only you had called the ambulance an hour earlier, *if only* you had persuaded Mom to give up her job last year, *if only* you had been able to push your parents into moving to a better climate, they could have been saved. Surely there must have been something you could have done?

Survivor guilt deals with the fact that we still consider ourselves responsible and powerful in the face of death, even though all the evidence proves otherwise. When we're used to making life better by our own efforts, it's hard to let go and admit there was absolutely nothing we could do.

This kind of guilt can be less potent after a parent's death because it is natural for parents to die before their children. Our guilt that our father has gone may be heightened by a certain relief that it was his generation's turn and not ours.

Linked to this is a certain uneasy feeling that your own need to live somehow contributed to your parent's death. This is called the *pelican complex*, after the idea that pelican youth allegedly drink their mother's blood. Maria was particularly conscious of this feeling.

> ⁊ "Until Mom got sick, I was eager to get married and have a baby. We had a wedding date all lined up, but she didn't live to see the wedding. I feel kind of superstitious about my plans, as if by planning my life, I was being too selfish for her. My plans, my wanting to move ahead, took too much of her energy.
>
> "When she was finishing with life, I seemed to be just starting my own. I had a need to live, she had a need to die. Neither of us could change, but the contrast made me feel guilty."

The fact that a parent's death removes the buffering generation between ourselves and death can also mean that guilt blends into fear. Thoughts of "it might be me next" or "it could have been me" are common.

You may have to come to terms with guilt over "not being good enough" as a child. The child's self-centeredness can be profound—that feeling that you're somehow responsible for

You may have to come to terms with guilt over "not being good enough" as a child.

everything and that if your father is in a bad mood, you caused it.

After your father's death, memories take on a special sting. All the times you stayed out late or didn't do well at school or ran with the wrong crowd, all the quarrels, the resentments and the fault-finding take on added weight.

Try to keep this in proportion. Some rebellion is a healthy part of growing up. If there were genuine personality problems, guilt can both cloud the issue and keep you paralyzed. Although guilt is a powerful emotion, it doesn't necessarily spur you into moving ahead or sorting out personal problems. As with most other stalemates in grief, talking with someone you trust can help.

You have had a profound influence on your parents, but remember that this influence is limited. Also, keep in mind that our parents are probably more tolerant of us and our shortcomings than anyone else. In addition to feeling guilty about the life we shared as parents and children, however, many feel guilty about the time *during* the death. Little things may bother you for years.

> ᘔ Anita always regretted that when the ambulance arrived to take her mother to the hospital, she hadn't gone back for the book her mother was reading at the time because she didn't want to ask the driver to wait. Anita's guilt was mixed with deep sadness. At this stage, neither she nor her mother knew that this trip would be her mother's last.

Anxiety

Anxiety takes many forms, including physical. What has happened to the person who was first responsible for your safety can make you feel unsafe in a profound way.

You may experience insomnia. You may feel it isn't safe to go to sleep, that it might be possible for you too to drift off into death as soon as unconsciousness comes. Of course, you may not experience anything as definite as this. You may think you just have too much on your mind to sleep. These sleepless nights in which you don't feel like reading or doing anything can be truly miserable. If you can't sleep, at least rest.

What has happened to the person who was first responsible for your safety can make you feel unsafe in a profound way.

You may feel like your body can't be trusted, that it will fall apart on you at any moment. Exercise and taking care of yourself can help combat these feelings about your physical body.

If your mother has died, concern with your own body may stem from the fact that you came out of your mother's body, the one that has ceased to function. If you lose weight after the death, it can be easy to fear you're becoming skeletal and you may not share such a thought for fear of being labeled *neurotic*.

Although such thoughts are natural, it is important not to give in to them. Swimming a few laps or jogging a few blocks can convince you of your physical health and can help you avoid some of the manifestations of physical grief.

Physical Grief

Although grief is not an illness but a normal life event, it is possible to experience it physically. Grief absorbs large amounts of energy, leaving you run-down and more vulnerable to illness. In particular, you may feel symptoms that mimic the disease your parent died from.

> After Heather's father died of bowel cancer, she began experiencing stomach problems: loss of appetite, constipation and diarrhea. Luckily, her doctor saw that her increased visits were related to her father's death. Once Heather understood this, she was able to accept and improve her health.
>
> She also had to make an effort to eat well, something she found difficult after watching her father's appetite diminish over the weeks. Panic attacks were another symptom of her grief.
>
> After she sorted out her major health problems, Heather never thought to connect her grief with other symptoms, such as not breathing right and feeling a lump in her throat. She sometimes felt so giddy that her head felt like it was spinning. Again, it took hospital tests to make her understand that these were also manifestations of grief, in this case delayed for a few months after her father's death.

Be sure to check out such symptoms with your doctor if you are worried. You may need medical help.

Going Off Course?

Your progress through life is interrupted dramatically by a parent's death. The first couple years of mourning can sometimes take the form of what traditional spiritualists call the *dark night of the soul:* a period of emptiness, dryness or bleakness. All life and all hope seem suspended. Only much later can you see any value in this period when apparent spiritual indifference actually covers new growth. During this time, people may go off course for a while, making uncharacteristic decisions, such as taking a job that's not right for them.

> ⟅ Colin, a flamboyant actor, quit acting after his mother's death and started teaching in a dull girls' school, which his friends thought was totally out of character. Later, this experience was something of a mystery to Colin. He could only explain it in terms of his need for isolation after his mother's death. Because of the raw sensitivity of those first two years, Colin couldn't bear the public pretense of his profession. He just wanted to put his head down and hide from the world as much as possible.

Delayed Grief

Grief that you don't live through completely can stop you from moving ahead. With our cultural fear of expressing emotion, you may feel unprepared for the overwhelming force of your grief. It seems to demand too much for too long and the changes it initiates are too sweeping.

Grief demands that we move on from the life we once had and try to deal with the challenges of new situations. This is enough to frighten some people into not facing grief at all. You may feel an urge to stay put as much as possible, even though new lives and new selves await those who can face their pain.

If you don't fully grieve for your parent at the time, this grief may strike later during another loss.

Other factors can delay grieving, especially important life events, such as getting married and having children. If you don't fully grieve for your parent at the time, this grief may strike later during another loss. This can happen as much as twenty or thirty years later, perhaps when a spouse dies.

Pregnancy

According to some researchers, pregnancy can produce a unique time when normal mourning reactions are impossible. A woman is said to be so preoccupied with the new life within that she cannot focus on the death of a parent enough to grieve.

What is happening in her own body is too extreme in its opposition to death. Problems then start after the birth, often with postnatal depression compounded by not having your parent around to support you as much as you had expected. Certainly, there is a special pain in not being able to share your new life with the person who gave you life.

> ⚶ Michelle learned she was pregnant in the morning. In the evening she hurried to the hospital to tell her mother, only to find that she had already died.

Remember, pregnancy and birth are times of unpredictable emotions; the "correct" feelings may not surface after a birth. You will experience natural mourning processes during pregnancy anyway, as you say goodbye to the self you were, leave behind a familiar life and embark on the unknown. This process intensifies after birth as you adjust to your new role.

If you suffer from postnatal depression, something that can be worsened by unresolved grief, remember it is treatable. Ask for help from your doctor or contact a special support group.

Taking a Break from Grieving

Grieving is hard work and, as with any work, you need time off. This usually occurs naturally. You forget for a day or so, and then it all comes flooding back. Still, you should try to cultivate the ability to put grief aside from time to time. It is not being disloyal to your parent—those memories will always be with you.

> *Grieving is hard work and, as with any work, you need time off.*

Discipline yourself to go for a walk instead of sitting around, to seek company when you know you are strong enough to handle it, or do something simple like painting the kitchen. It is impossible to feel pure emotions for long periods of time.

A vacation helps some people, after the initial shock is over. Again, it isn't possible to predict a good time to take a vacation. Like everything else, it depends on your personal state. Going away enables you to devote time to people you've been neglecting because of your father's illness and death. Still, depending on your personal grief process, a vacation can make grief both more and less painful.

> Michael took his wife and children away a couple of months after his father died so they could all spend more time together. He found this restorative, and the beautiful scenery around them also helped. However, the pureness of nature also seemed to act as a pure channel for his grief and he felt heartsick in a way he hadn't when surrounded by the daily distractions of everyday life.
>
> The whole family enjoyed this time together. It was a break in which they could settle down and start to think about their own lives again, both the present and the future.

6

Loss Patterns

FOUR MAIN FACTORS AFFECT THE WAY you react to your loss:

1. How your parent died—sudden death is more of a shock than gradual death (although no less painful)
2. The quality of your relationship with your parent
3. The support you have during grief
4. Your past experience with loss

Also consider your own life situation: If your life is still evolving, or is involved with other significant events, that can affect mourning. Chapter 5 traces the basic outline of grief; this chapter looks at influences on grief and at the nature of loss.

There's a fine line between *normal* and *complicated* grief. Grief feels so abnormal anyway, crashing into your life, destroying your assumptions and plans. People's lives are seldom simple enough to make the death of a mother or father the only event in them. People move, have babies, have car accidents, have problems at work, worry about debt and so on. But your life situation can complicate your mourning. Other deaths, major life events, quirks in your own personality or unresolved complications in your relationship with your dead mother or father can all make grief last longer or be more complicated.

If this sounds depressing, the positive side is that these added problems often spur you to take the initiative, to push your problems over the edge of an old life as you move into a new one. If asked in advance, we would probably say we just wouldn't be able to bear it, but people not only bear grief, they even triumph under a combination of events they would have previously thought of as catastrophic.

The Nature of Loss

Every stage of life involves loss in some form or another. Every move forward means leaving something behind. The child who goes to a babysitter's or to school leaves the security of home—the first separation from your mother can be important in determining

Every stage of life involves loss in some form or another.

your reactions to later losses. The babysitter and school are not necessarily negative experiences; such events are often life-enhancing. It's just that going there means leaving the established routine behind and a certain pattern of life is gone forever.

The same happens when we move—perhaps more so in childhood when we aren't the ones choosing to move. Many new experiences lie ahead, but it means leaving old ones behind. The same is true of marriage, which is one reason why many people find marriage more difficult than they anticipated.

Pregnancy and the arrival of children bring their own special, if temporary, grief as you leave one part of your life behind and assume the status and responsibilities of parenthood. In all such life situations, a lot is gained, but a lot is also lost.

This raises questions about the value and meaning of loss. If every gain means a loss, could this be turned around? Can loss bring gain? These are important questions because they focus on a major thrust of this book: moving ahead toward maturity. One of the difficulties in answering such questions, certainly in early bereavement, is that just to ask them can raise a storm of guilt and grief.

No matter how relieved we may be to see a long drawn-out death terminated at last, our relief is usually that our parent's suffering is over. And we ourselves are released from the intolerable strain of watching a deathbed. That such a relief could have long-term implications doesn't seem important immediately after death.

Besides, if loss constitutes gain, it isn't a gain that we choose—it's forced on us. We would never dream of changing ourselves the way this experience changes us. At the beginning of our loss, it is not possible to see the kind of people we will become as a result of it. As always, we have to take our future growth on trust.

> *As always, we have to take our future growth on trust.*

Other Losses Soon after Your Parent's Death

Having to go through two bereavements around the same time can prolong mourning. You may feel numb to one, unable to believe or understand it, or it may jolt you into mourning the earlier death in a way you are not yet able to cope with.

> ⚭ Anita lost her grandmother a few months after losing her mother. She had been close to her grandmother and felt that this really was a goodbye to her childhood and to any mothering she might expect.

The death of a pet can be just as devastating, a real tragedy in some people's lives and, in a few cases, an escape from the other death that has occurred.

> ⚭ Susan's cat was hit by a car within weeks of her father's death. People who saw her after it happened were shocked by her incredible grief for the animal, which seemed to put aside any grief for her father. She kept worrying and talking loudly about how much pain the cat had suffered and how long it probably lay at the side of the road before being discovered by a neighbor and taken to the veterinarian. Susan said the cat had been so much a part of her life that she almost felt as if she had lost a baby.

This is an example of how grief can be deflected. We focus on the smaller loss because the other one is too big for us to deal with just yet. The same mechanism can operate with other losses that occur soon after a parent's death. We may feel an unusual amount of sadness at failing an exam, losing a job or breaking a friendship.

> ~€ Jackie's friends were surprised at how she reacted to a break-up with a new boyfriend. The relationship had barely gotten started, yet she was extremely upset about it. Then one friend, more observant and braver than the rest, told her she was probably mourning her father's recent death more than losing her boyfriend.

The departure of certain hopes can call for mourning, too. The death of a parent usually leaves us in search of a new identity. But what happens if the role we hoped to fill is kept from us?

> ~€ Ruth, whose mother died unexpectedly in an accident, had to face another loss at the same time. She was told she would not be able to have a baby, after years of waiting and taking countless infertility tests. Her mourning job was doubled. Not only did she have to grieve for her mother, but for the motherhood she herself would never have, for the children she would never bear.

Ruth's story is an example of how the death of a parent can be the death of the past, ending a chapter in our lives. Along with other circumstances, a parent's death can effectively cut your life in two, resulting in a completely new set of circumstances.

> ~€ As a nurse, Ruth's infertility, combined with the terrible shock of her mother's death, had affected her in other ways. She no longer wanted to work with other people's children and she also wanted to move. She and her husband had bought a large house with acreage a few years previously because they thought they would soon be having a family.
>
> Although Ruth could not accept her situation entirely, she was strong enough to rise above it. She and her husband moved to a smaller place and Ruth changed careers, accepting a high-powered executive position for a large charity.

It's important to remember that such changes don't happen all at once. You may still need to go through the exhausting process of grief before you have the energy to initiate such moves. Don't try to force the pace. In the scheme of things, a year or two is not that long in such major transitions.

Earlier Loss

Your progress through bereavement is affected by your experience of loss during childhood. Because a parent's death can so easily make us feel like children again, it quickly triggers the fear, anguish and helplessness we felt before. This could happen when faced with the death of a grandmother or news that your father left home because of divorce or death and isn't coming back.

Your progress through bereavement is affected by your experience of loss during childhood.

But loss in childhood may not be anything this drastic. It may have to do with losing a pet, moving, going to school or enduring the temporary absence of one or both parents. The definitions of loss are varied and individual. Whatever the loss, you feel it more deeply in childhood, partly because children don't have that much power over their lives.

Even without the desolation caused by the death of a parent, loss can bring a feeling of emptiness, of romance or glory passing away, that we don't yet have the experience to handle.

> Heather was deeply disillusioned at ten when her grandparents moved from their home in the country to a place in the city. She lost a huge, overgrown garden and adjoining field—a child's garden of paradise—and the freedom to wander through the surrounding countryside. She also lost a pair of grandparents who up until then had been the keepers of a fairy-tale place for Heather to escape to.

An important feature of loss in childhood can be how our parents helped us deal with it, even how they can be implicated in or the cause of it. Such memories can be revealing and it is worth emphasizing that the loss itself may not actually be a major one.

> ᓚ When Anita was a young child, her mother
> threw out a ragged and dirty doll. Anita vividly
> recalls her sense of misery when she saw the
> doll disappearing into the garbage can.

Although trivial from an adult viewpoint, this incident was significant because it was bound to the general sense of frustration she experienced in her relationship with her mother. It wasn't the event, but the way it was conducted. Of course, the expectations of children and their parents seldom match—neither side can get it right all the time. Nevertheless, Anita analyzed the doll incident after her mother's death.

> ᓚ "It created a feeling that my mother was in
> charge of loss, like a god—pretty scary. Even more
> frightening was to see her dying and realize it just
> wasn't true. You don't realize you have these lifelong
> assumptions about your parents and the way they
> behave, until they die."

An ongoing insensitivity or clumsiness about a child's feelings, a lack of awareness of how they experience loss, can become an unspoken part of the parent-child relationship, leaving inevitable repercussions when the parents die.

> ᓚ Michael remembers how his father, Tom, messed
> things up when a favorite family dog had to be put
> to sleep. First, Tom didn't tell the family for two days
> but let them assume the dog had wandered away.
> Then he got drunk and blurted the news out in tears
> until most of the family were also in tears.
> Memories of this pathetic incident returned to
> Michael at Tom's deathbed, adding to his feeling
> that Tom was not really equipped to deal with his
> own death.

Loss of a parent in childhood

What happens if you lose a parent in adulthood after losing one in childhood? This partly depends on how well adults handled the earlier loss and how completely you lived through the grief at the time. Adults who underestimate how much a child can understand may be tempted to gloss over the death. As a result, the child is deprived of valuable support in working through his grief.

> *Adults who underestimate how much a child can understand may be tempted to gloss over the death.*

ℛ Jonathan was told that his mother had gone away for a while, but she had really been killed in a car crash when he was seven. Therefore he locked his grief inside because he didn't think he was supposed to feel it, and some of this grief permeated his entire life. As an adult, he rarely spoke about his mother, saying there was no need to and that her loss hadn't affected his life.

He was absolutely stiff-lipped, dogmatically matter-of-fact, tending to say, "Everything will be all right," even when facts suggested otherwise. It was only when his father died that Jonathan was forced to realize that he had double mourning to do—his father's loss triggered the feelings of desolation and loneliness he had experienced at his mother's loss but that he had never worked through.

The loss of a parent in childhood is one of life's better-studied tragedies. Many researchers have pointed out how damaging the long-term effects can be, especially if it happened when the child was under ten. Effects can include low self-esteem, depression and nervous breakdown. Some believe that too much emphasis on this is unfair to those who were bereaved in such a way. Focusing on the adverse effects doesn't really take into account a person's potential for recovery and growth. (For more information about losing a parent or other loved person in childhood, see Further Reading in the back of this book.)

The death of other family members

If other family members died during your childhood, your security may not be undermined in the same way as when a parent dies. Nevertheless, even a distant relation's death changes both the world as you knew it and your emotional status. While an earlier death can help prepare you for your parent's death, it doesn't help with the grief. Perhaps the shock isn't as great as it might have been.

> By the time her mother died, Maria had also lost two grandparents, an aunt and a school friend. In realizing that death was a part of life, she felt she had acquired some valuable knowledge, even though this was no consolation when her mother died. But, after a while, she found it comforting to think that so many people had gone ahead of her mother and that death was not an uninhabited country.

This depends on your beliefs about afterlife, but while the death of a parent removes the buffer between you and death, it can be reassuring to think of a loved one having accomplished what yet lies ahead of you.

It can be reassuring to think of a loved one having accomplished what yet lies ahead of you.

Loss of a sibling can be another factor that affects your attitude toward your parent's death.

> Clare's childhood was overshadowed by the death of her brother when she was ten. Clare's parents always upheld him as a bright, promising boy, a shining star against which she couldn't hope to compete. When her parents died within a few weeks of each other, all her former feelings of sorrow, guilt and rage were renewed.
>
> She was also conscious of a certain relief: Her parents had gone to join her brother at last and she was free to live her own life, instead of bearing the burden of their sorrow and thwarted expectations.

What if you were lied to about death as a child? Parents use different ways of explaining death to children at different ages. For example, a very young child might need to visualize death as a different country far away. But if you weren't told the truth about death at an age when you could have accepted a more mature explanation, this can add to the unease and mystery of the event when your mother or father dies.

> ⚔ Guy lost an aunt when he was about twelve. His parents told him it was from a heart attack. Many years later Guy discovered that it had been suicide. When the little-white-lies technique was used later, as his father was dying, this earlier incident added to Guy's anger and grief.

Not telling the whole truth about death can be part of a more general situation in which parents aren't really honest with their children.

Divorce or separation

As discussed above, a parent's death can trigger the pain of a specific loss that happened earlier in life. This may be the loss caused by separation or divorce in a family when one of the parents moves out of the child's day-to-day life.

He or she may not actually be dead, but it's a kind of death to the child, who sees far less of one parent on a day-to-day basis. Certainly the only family life the child knew has passed away.

> ⚔ Julia's mother and father had been divorced since she was eleven. When Julia's father, Martin, became ill at the age of seventy-seven, her mother reacted by having a slight stroke or some kind of nervous breakdown. The doctor's uncertainty about the diagnosis didn't help at this traumatic time.
>
> Julia's mother retreated into the past and became difficult to manage. When Julia's father eventually died a few years later, Julia was hit with the need to mourn not only his passing, but also the earlier loss created by divorce.

(Continued...)

> The pervading sense of silence and desolation in
> the house, a sense of being horribly cut off from the
> outside world, of having her life interrupted and not
> being able to start it again, were just as powerful
> at her father's death as when he had left all those
> years earlier.

Such an experience poses a frightening threat to your identity.
To have events return you to the unhappy past can leave you
with the feeling that all the years in between, with their many
achievements, were for nothing. You may feel that you've hardly
moved ahead at all from the pain and confusion of earlier loss.

Perhaps you mainly need to allow yourself to feel these
feelings—all of them. Anger and bewilderment do not make for
comfortable living, but the prospect of them is often more
frightening than actually experiencing them. If you let them run
their course, you will discover that they have limits, but you may
need support to do this. Another person, probably a trained
counselor, can act as a valuable safety net.

Earlier loss can also sour your relationship with your surviving
parent. It's hard to avoid the good-bad syndrome in divorce, and
Julia was left feeling bitterly angry with her mother for what she
saw as a habit of escaping, first through divorce and then through
illness. Julia felt that her mother left her and her sister with the
entire burden of coping on their own.

Parents and prison

When a parent goes to prison, as with a violent or abusive parent,
you may need to mourn what you *never* had—a strong, supportive
parent and a stable family life.

> ᴦ Mary never got over her father going to prison
> when she was nine. Her security was shattered for
> life. She might have gotten over the isolated incident,
> but he repeated his offense (stealing) and was jailed
> a few more times until Mary was in her teens, when
> he managed to stop stealing with the help of a good
> prison psychiatrist.

In later life, Mary was able to understand her father's actions as attention-seeking behavior caused by unhappiness. She was able to overcome the emotional scars to a large extent, but she could never entirely erase them.

Later, her father's death evoked the same reactions she'd had when he had gone to prison. When her father departed, the home order was upset and the house felt less safe. There was also the social stigma, the feeling that she was cut off from other normal people.

Losing Your Mother or Father Early in Life

The definition of *early in life* depends to a large extent not on age but on the stage you have reached in life. A twenty-one-year-old who's happily married, with a job or a baby, may feel further along in life than a twenty-nine-year-old who hasn't met the right man yet or isn't sure of the direction of her career. Your maturity depends on what you have yet to achieve and how dependent you have been emotionally or materially on your parent.

> *Your maturity depends on what you have yet to achieve and how dependent you have been emotionally or materially on your parent.*

꙰ At twenty-two, Guy felt that he couldn't have lost his father at a worse time. He was about to leave college to start out in life and he needed his father to talk with about all the decisions that faced him. Also, his father had promised him some letters of introduction to friends of his, with the idea that Guy might have been able to find a job with some of them. So, Guy felt his father's death narrowed his horizons in more ways than one.

Guy took a job in the same town where his mother lived for a while. He didn't get along with his boss, whose abrasive attitude contributed to the somber mood of the next year. In Guy's case, the problems so many graduates experience in their first job were a considerable factor in his unhappiness about his father. He also felt that he was indulging in selfishness and in immature dependency. From this point of view, however, all grief is selfish and it is natural to want a parent's support when starting out in life.

If you lose your parent early in your life, chances are that it's relatively early in *their* lives, before the expected sixty-plus age bracket. This involves what could be called *unselfish* grief—mourning the opportunities you feel your parent has lost, for the years he will never live and the plans he will never fulfill.

> ⟿ Guy's father, Edward, had married young and was only forty-seven. His death interrupted not only his career as a business consultant, but all sorts of other plans. Now that Guy and the other children were grown up, Edward and his wife had planned to travel and possibly buy a second home in a vacation spot. Guy was bitterly sorry to see those plans gone.

Grief for Your Parent's Life

Mourning for what should have been the dead parent's future also leads to mourning about their past—an area where it is probably wise not to empathize with your parent's life. We simply don't know all the facts, and our grief may give us a distorted picture of our parents' past, especially at first.

> ⟿ Guy now felt that his father had spent his whole life working terribly hard, without ever quite reaping the rewards of his labors or achieving his full potential. In the same way, Michael mourned the personality difficulties that had prevented his father from living as full a life as he might have.

In this mood, it is easy to feel that your parent's life was futile, narrow, pathetic, nothing but a race for money, a race against time.

Time brings a fuller picture. Guy was later able to see his father's life as busy, valuable and contented, despite the fact that his father kept things to himself. Michael also saw that Tom, with his ferocious sense of humor, had gotten a lot of fun out of his seventy-two years, despite his constant dissatisfaction.

> *Time brings a fuller picture.*

Any death leads you to question what a life has been for, and the death of your mother or father is no exception. Give yourself time for a more positive picture to emerge, to counteract the rather bleak "Was that all?" feeling of earlier mourning.

In the long term, *not* judging is more useful than being too contemplative about a life that was not yours, whose details you will never fully know.

Seeking Substitute Parents

Looking for someone to replace your parent is a strong if unconscious urge that is more likely to strike if you were bereaved early in life. You may become closer to an aunt or uncle, or to grandparents who are still alive, although it is often easier to find someone outside the family.

> Anita struggled with dependency when she befriended an older woman in her office. In the desperate loneliness following her mother's death, Anita could not help attaching herself to her friend, accompanying her to stores at lunchtime and talking to her perhaps too much about her fears and her future.
>
> Anita treated her as a younger person would have treated her mother. In the end, Anita felt guilty about taking her kindly friend's energy and time, and this feeling was one of the main things that spurred her into getting another job. It took Anita many years and some counseling to get over her tendency to depend on others.

This may seem like a rather grim future of working again and again through the weaknesses left by a parent's death, but such work is not a waste of time, even if it seems to be getting you nowhere at the time.

> ⫷ Anita eventually found herself in the happy position of being able to give as well as take, with a responsible job and an established if not sometimes tempestuous relationship. "It had to be worked through" was her comment on the years of grief and uncertainty following her mother's death. "It wasn't even that I'm stronger because of it. I'm just a different person. At least that's how I see myself."

How Much Guilt and Anger?

Guilt takes many forms: that gnawing self-blame that tells us we could have done something to prevent the death; the focus on all the little ways in which we may have failed to make our dying parent's last weeks and days more comfortable.

In time, a more balanced outlook usually emerges; we are able to forgive not only the event but ourselves, to see that we did all we could. We see that our failures were more than outweighed by the loving intentions and anxious care we managed to give, and by the pain and helplessness we experienced at their suffering.

However, if guilt was a strong part of the relationship with your parents before their death, you may need to do more work before finally laying it to rest. Guilt can also be a way of holding on to the event or trying to control it.

You know where you stand with guilt.

Its range, if limited, is at least defined. You know where you stand with guilt. Sometimes you must be ruthless to throw away what has become a comfort and move on. In the end, prolonged guilt is a refusal to accept that we are powerless over cancer, car accidents and death itself.

You can fight guilt by recognizing if it is inappropriate and by putting yourself in a new mindset. To do this, try the exercise in the box opposite.

Working through Guilt

1. Write down a list of your guilty feelings (which probably look a lot less imposing on paper).

2. In a column alongside, write down what you actually did for your parent as well as the tender feelings you had.

3. Focus on the positive list (from step 2), which should be longer than the negative.

4. Be firm about pushing away guilty thought patterns and replacing them with new, more positive ones.

What about anger? It is important to distinguish between the anger of bereavement and the lifelong unresolved anger of some difficult relationships.

> Michael was an angry man, always chomping at the bit in life, perhaps because he was used to finding and expressing this emotion within himself. His father's death allowed him to express the sorrow and fear behind his anger and he actually coped quite well with his anger in bereavement.

> Maria was normally a quiet, caring girl, but after her mother's death, she experienced strange rages that gradually decreased in intensity.

It is not fair to blame yourself for feeling too much, or to be afraid of your rage. Until it happens, you may not know just how much anger the event has created in you, or how bitter and all-encompassing it may be on some days. If you are worried by the depth or strength of your feelings, talk to someone else who has been through bereavement. Knowing that someone else has gone through it too can make a big difference when it comes to forgiving yourself afterward.

Estranged Children

What if you were not talking to your parents for months or years before their deaths? This might be because of an argument, because you've been living far away or simply because life has taken you in different directions. How you react to the death depends on the reason why you haven't been seeing them.

It is possible to lose touch with parents just as we do with other people: our interests aren't the same, we don't have that much to say to each other, the relationship seems to have run its course or any number of reasons.

If the separation was one of avoidance because of relationship problems, then grief will probably include a larger share of guilt and uncertainty about your identity.

> ⌇ Melanie had made a life for herself in Mexico as an English teacher. She'd just had her first baby. She was expecting her mother to come for a long visit when the news came that her mother had died. Sorting out their complicated relationship was something Melanie had always hoped to do.

She had been even more firmly resolved to do it now that she was a mother herself. Melanie hadn't realized how much her attitude toward her mother had been a focus in her life, something to react against. "I would always say, 'at least I'm not like Mom, I haven't stayed in the same boring place.' Suddenly, that prop was gone."

Such a job now has to be done alone, with all the accompanying regrets at the wasted opportunities of the past, and all the confusion. You must mourn the relationship that never was, or that could have been. You miss out on that chance to say goodbye that is so important. How you handle this depends on individual circumstances.

> ⌇ Melanie went to Canada with her baby to see her mother's grave and meet relatives she hadn't seen for years. This process helped her shed some of her grief because she felt she was facing the issue squarely for the first time.

"I was able to accept that Mom and I never did agree and probably never would have, no matter what. She wanted me to be someone different. I wanted her to be someone different. I hope now we can leave each other in peace!"

Sometimes, especially if the parent was estranged, it may be just a question of acceptance, an attitude that may come slowly and painfully.

ぞ Because of the family quarrel, Michael's father had seen very little of Michael's wife and their children. Part of Michael's grief was coming to terms with the way the feud had overshadowed his family life this way.

How Death Can Spur Bad Behavior

A parent's death can sometimes trigger latent problems, or make existing ones worse. This is especially true if it happens earlier instead of later in life while you are still relying on your parents to help you out whenever you get into trouble. Although a parent's death means a painful period for the child, it can also have the good effect of forcing a crisis. This type of reaction can push a person into a complete reappraisal of his whole life.

ぞ Nicholas, already a heavy drinker, let his father's death spur him into an alarming dependence on alcohol. He had previously relied on his father, Graham, to rescue him from the results of his binges. Graham would often pay his debts and, more importantly, talk him through the guilt and remorse that followed one of Nicholas's binges.
Now that Graham was dead, Nicholas experienced many problems, culminating two years later in the loss of his job and his wife leaving. Nicholas was forced to overcome his problem on his own. Initially he relied on group and individual therapy, but he eventually moved away from both.

(Continued . . .)

In fact, in later years, he sometimes wondered if he would ever have managed his painful crawl to true independence if his father had still been alive.

Nicholas is an example of delayed grieving. Giving up drinking was the hardest thing he ever had to do in his life. It was even harder than losing his father because, without alcohol, he had to face the emptiness and hurt completely for the first time.

His story also underscores the dangers of turning to comforters such as alcohol and cigarettes after a parent's death. They may provide temporary relief, but they can't permanently remove the need to grieve.

You may also later regret unfinished business. After the death, what can be done? Perhaps for a long time you can't do much. The most mature course is simply to live with this knowledge. If you recognize the personality problem and attempt to change, you may be able to resolve the unfinished business with yourself later.

> ❧ More mature and stable seven years after his father's death, Nicholas was able to help his new wife through the death of her mother. He was present at the death. He had avoided his own father's deathbed and felt in this way he was making up for all the neglected responsibilities that had been too much for him to handle with his own father.

If Death Is a Relief

Death often is an immediate relief. When an illness has dragged on and on, you welcome the end. But that first thankful feeling that it's over at last doesn't make it any easier to lose the person. You can be glad for them, but not for you.

But that first thankful feeling that it's over at last doesn't make it any easier to lose the person.

What if you are glad to be finally rid of a parent? What if your own feelings toward your parents have been largely mixed with confusion and hatred or if death rids the family of a bad-tempered bully or an emotional vampire? This isn't to say that you don't love a parent who is less than perfect, or a parent who plays all sorts of mind games with you.

> Anita was always uncomfortable because her mother, while urging her to be sociable, didn't like her to invite her friends to the house. Michael's father was completely unreasonable in terms of what he demanded from the family and what he gave back. Yet both were wholeheartedly loved within their family circle.

This does not refer to the normal feelings of ambivalence, that combination of exasperation and love that is always found in a family, or those remorseful thoughts of how you could have done better.

Instead it refers to a parent who has been an obvious problem, who terrorized the family for years with emotional unreliability or physical violence. In those sad cases when there has been verbal or physical abuse, the death of a mother or father can make adult children feel safer than ever before.

You also must mourn the relationship you never had, the father or mother you would have loved to have loved.

You experience no less grief in this situation. Recovery from bereavement depends on the quality of the relationship you had. The complications of a poor relationship can make for a lot of soul-searching after the death. You also must mourn the relationship you never had, the father or mother you would have loved to have loved.

> Kathy's father had regularly beaten her as a child, and she grew up with the single ambition of getting away. When she was an independent, successful working woman, she kept her address and phone number secret from him.
>
> Yet she dreaded his possible death because she knew it would be the end of any possibility of a reasonable relationship. When he died of liver

(Continued ...)

failure, her overwhelming relief was only the beginning of years of working through this painful and complicated relationship. Like Nicholas, Kathy needed a lot of support in this process.

Prolonged Grief

It's hard to put a limit on prolonged grief, but be suspicious if grief has become a way of life after two years, something of a sacred ritual. Prolonged grief is different from working through the long-term effects and implications of a parent's death, especially if it has happened earlier in life.

Maria, for example, estimated that it took her seven years to come completely to terms with her mother's death. Guy, some ten years later, had never really gotten over his father's death. But, in the interim, both pursued careers, married and had children. They went on living full lives while sorting out the aftermath of their grief.

If that darkness doesn't lift at all, if you start to feel overburdened with taking care of your surviving parent or simply unable to start your life again, consider professional help or consult a grief support organization.

7

Inheritance: New Possessions, New Ideas?

INHERITANCE HAS A BROAD MEANING in the context of a parent's death. Material and spiritual inheritance are closely intertwined. Can it ever be just *material* gain? The clock inherited from your father, and perhaps from his father before him, has far more value than one you buy for yourself.

Because inherited objects are so emotionally loaded, it is difficult to be objective about them. This is a reason why family fights over property appear so out of proportion to outsiders.

The inheritance of possessions or money may bring strong feelings of ambivalence. You may feel wrong that you now own what was recently another person's property. You may at times feel like you're intruding, especially if you have to go through things soon after the death, when the presence of your dead parent still seems strong.

You may have feelings of fear and sadness at how death scattered the structure of a lifetime. All the records, books and pictures so carefully collected over the years, which helped make a home, have now lost their essential value.

> *Deciding what to keep is a vital part of coming to terms with your parent's death and of forging your own new identity.*

Deciding what to keep is a vital part of coming to terms with your parent's death and of forging your own new identity. It's important to remember that, despite the sentimental value of the things your parent accumulated over the years, *you are not obliged to hang on to any of them.* What you keep can dictate how much of their lifestyle and personality you want to continue and how much you want to strike out on your own.

Also keep in mind the inheritance of *ideas*: what you've inherited not just from your family, but in a wider sense from society. If you were brought up in some form of religion, you may re-examine your thoughts and feelings on the subject. After a death, it is common for people to either turn to religion in the search for meaning, or to turn away feeling it has failed them.

Also, fully accepting a parent's death involves accepting the reality of your *own* mortality. At some point, you may benefit from thinking through your ideas about death in general. The event is bound to trigger reflection. The conclusions you come to will be more developed than your previous ideas. This can be a time to throw out ideas that have been handed down to you or go back to them and revise your cultural inheritance to fit your own particular style.

Losing a Part of Yourself

Losing a parent means losing a part of yourself, the flesh from which you came, if nothing else. But it's more than that. You've lost someone who was greatly responsible for the molding of your identity. You may even have depended on the identity that your father had of you, based on his definition of you.

You've also lost the person who had prime access to your childhood, who could pass on family memories and who knew, perhaps uniquely, how you'd changed and developed. This can leave you unexpectedly blank about your earlier years. You've lost the person who could fill in all the details of those classic family episodes: the Thanksgiving Grandma burned herself cooking the turkey, the real reasons behind the old argument your parents had with your aunt and uncle.

Losing a parent means losing a part of yourself.

You might also want to know some personal details that you were never told, like what time you were born, how often you threw tantrums as a child or at what age you learned to read. Such questions often become more important when you have children because of the natural urge to compare your children's development to your own in your early years. Or your children may ask questions about your childhood.

> *You go on changing and developing in many ways after a parent dies.*

A surviving parent can't always supply this information. Maybe he doesn't remember and perhaps you don't like to ask in case it raises memories of happier times. Fathers are often less specific about childhood details than mothers, who usually spent more time with their children when they were young. If you've lost both parents, this knowledge is probably lost forever.

Remember: Your identity isn't dependent on your parents, even if they first developed it. In the end, it is up to you to pick and choose which parts of that identity you want to carry forward into maturity. This may mean rejecting pieces of family myth ("Anita's so impractical—can't boil an egg." "Guy would never make a good husband—his head's always in the clouds.").

You go on changing and developing in many ways after a parent dies. The death itself can easily spur you into outgrowing family labels. This is especially true if one or both of your parents died while you were still establishing your adult identity.

Something to Keep?

Deciding what to keep and what not to keep is an important process after your parent's death. In the rawness of grief, you may want to shove everything out of sight, get rid of everything in the unconscious hope that you can sweep away some of your pain with it.

However, mementos acquire more value with the years, and what causes you pain in the beginning will be a precious link in the future. Try to make sure you have something to keep, however small. This can sometimes be difficult. It is common for people not to make wills, and even if they do, they often leave out minor keepsakes.

In this case, you may have to negotiate with other family members to obtain a memento. There's also the possibility that your surviving parent doesn't think of your need in this respect and you may be afraid of asking for fear of being thought selfish, greedy or intrusive.

> ᕙ Guy particularly wanted his father's watch, which his father received from his own father. However, his mother put all his father's possessions in a closet and shut the door. Three years later, his sister finally took everything when their mother was moving to an apartment. Guy was living in another part of the country and no one thought to ask him if he wanted anything.

Going to the opposite extreme, *too much* may be handed on.

> ᕙ Michael was given practically everything his father owned because his brothers were wealthy enough to need no more than a token each. As the youngest son and father of a growing family, his brothers thought Michael needed it more. He ended up with suits of clothes, a second record player, TV and other furniture.
> "It was too much. Dad had such a strong presence. It was like having him in the house—I could almost see him there in his apartment, old and sick, listening to his records or whatever."
> Finally, Michael and his wife went through everything, chose a few special items to keep, and gave the rest away.

As this story shows, economic need may dictate which family member inherits more. In times gone by, inheritance was a major way of obtaining possessions. Today, we tend to buy what we need, saving up for a new bed rather than inheriting Grandma's old one.

Deciding what to get rid of can be just as important as deciding what to keep in saying goodbye to your dead parent and in establishing your new identity.

~{ Margaret's elderly mother had collected milk-
bottle caps. When she died and Margaret went to
clean out her house, the very first thing she did was
throw away every single bottle cap in the house!

The collection may have been valuable to someone else who
collected milk-bottle caps. While it might have taken some effort to
locate such collectors, there's usually some group or organization
interested in buying just about anything. Or, you may choose to
donate the collection.

This is a situation in which a discussion with your mother
about what she wanted done with her effects would have been
helpful before her death. If you know your father wanted all his
clothes sent to a charity, you have no decisions to make, and no
regrets later for making the wrong one. Giving away belongings
can also be a valuable part of the mourning process, although it
pays to wait a while before you decide what to part with.

~{ Heather gave away her father's old and valuable
collection of books and, at the same time, she gave
away all her own childhood books. She felt that if
she and Will ever had children, they would want to
start over, without the ghosts of family memories.
Later, when thinking more about a baby, she
regretted throwing out everything. She should have
kept some of her books for her own children.

Although it's usually a mistake to rush in and get rid of
everything, hanging on to belongings can sometimes hold you
back. Sorting through them helps you acknowledge the depth and
reality of what has happened, to clear both mental and physical
space for what is to come next.

Although it's a painful task, you need
to sort through the belongings before
they acquire a kind of taboo from
being left untouched.

*Look carefully at every
scrap of paper before
discarding it.*

If you have piles of papers and materials to sort through, do it
carefully. There are thousands of stories of unknown treasure that
suddenly surfaces in a dead person's effects.

It's certainly not unusual for records of forgotten bank accounts, certificates of deposit, stock certificates and other valuables to show up in files, books and piles of paper. Look carefully at every scrap of paper before discarding it. You could discover that your parent left you much more than you could have hoped for.

Benefiting from Inheritance

There is a grain of truth in detective novels and well-worn jokes about disposing of rich relatives in order to inherit. The dream of being given a large sum of money is why games of chance such as lotteries are so popular.

Yet, how can you legitimately feel glad about gaining extra money from the death of a parent? It is easy to feel ambivalent about bigger inheritances. They may raise many practical questions. For example, it is more common now to inherit property, even though the heirs may already own homes.

> When Jackie lost both parents, they left her a house and a lot of money. Never a career woman, she now didn't have to work—a rarity in today's society. It actually added to the sense of isolation she felt after her parents' death.
> As an only child, she had never been close to the rest of her family. At first she thought the money alienated other people even more. She was able to overcome these feelings in time with the help of an established circle of friends and a happy marriage.

If you are the only heir, you may find yourself either wealthier than you ever expected or burdened with paying off two mortgages or other debts. Even if you feel sure about it, think seriously before giving up your own home and moving into your parents' house. You may feel a strong desire to stay close to the family home during the first few weeks after the death, but if you make it a permanent arrangement, you may give up friends and connections that would be more valuable to you in the long run.

Sometimes inheritance can bring other changes in lifestyle, even if you don't become interested in them. You may inherit a business, or pieces of equipment that might give your career a new direction.

> ◞ Glen inherited his father's import business and, after some indecision, decided to run it himself instead of selling it.

> ◞ Colin inherited a computer he used to get a presentation-skills business off the ground— something he'd been thinking about to supplement the uncertain life (and income) of an actor.

But it may not always be appropriate to hang on to inheritances. They may be a link with a past that really has little meaning in your day-to-day life.

> ◞ Clare inherited a small farm. At first she was determined to run it, but it soon became clear that happy childhood memories of the farm were one thing, managing a business was another. Bigger farms were eager to buy her out. With her roots firmly in a large city, she decided that it made more sense to sell.

Your Inner Home

One of the most important long-term effects of losing a parent is that it leads you to find your own center—the inner home that gives you roots. Achieving emotional independence from our parents takes place whether they die or not, but it is inevitably easier when they do.

Stephen touched on this transition when speaking of his uncertainty about where his home was now that both parents were dead.

> ◞ "I eventually realized, after a few months, that it was up to me to make my own home now. I don't mean I rushed out and bought a place, just that I

had to get used to thinking of myself as the source
of security. There wasn't some long umbilical cord
trailing back home anymore. Not that there had
been before, only traces existed, but now even
the traces were gone."

Achieving your inner home marks the transition from being a
receiver (the child whose duty it is to accept) to a giver (the adult
whose duty it is to give). Passive becomes active and the person
who always attended family events may now become the one to
initiate them. You may change from going home every Christmas
as a guest to being the one out in the kitchen cooking the turkey
while the rest of the family relaxes in the next room.

Being settled in this way is a mark of the greater self-reliance
that comes after a parent's death, although it may not come all at
once but gradually over a period of years.

In this sense you become the *culture carrier* mentioned in
chapter 5. It is now up to you to decide whether you even want
to celebrate Christmas or not. There may be family traditions you
don't want to let slip or you may want to continue or even expand
on a parent's cultural interests.

You could enlarge a parent's record or book collection after
your mother or father is dead. This is possible because, in a sense,
they are no longer there to react against change. You may be
surprised by how much of their tradition you do wish to continue.

Habits you laughed at before, like regular Sunday lunch, not
only achieve a certain sentimental value but can become important
in their own right once you have freely chosen to do them.

Your New Perception of Death

An important part of the grieving process is to come to terms with
your new perception of death. This may take more than the couple
of years of initial mourning. Some preoccupation with death
(but only some) must always remain a part of any mature person's
concept of life. The knowledge of your mortality, once accepted,
can be a valuable spur toward setting goals in both work and play.

One writer suggested that without death we wouldn't bother to achieve or create and that art would have little meaning. Facing death can help free you for many enterprises, if only because you don't spend so much energy hiding from the fear of it.

First Death

For everyone there is a *first death*—the first time death becomes real to you. For many people, the first death is their parent's, so that they face the shock of losing someone so close *and* the shock of confronting the unknown, the void.

It's at this point you may see how much our society hides from death, making it invisible in spite of its apparent daily appearance in the media. It is quite possible for people to reach their forties and fifties without ever having seen a dead body.

In reaction, the enormous dark fact of death may seem like the only reality. Time will restore balance to your outlook, but it does take time to digest this new realization of death.

This isn't to say that you will always accept future deaths as matter of fact. Death is always death. But when it happens again, it may not seem quite so impossible. You will have become familiar with the effects of shock, grief and fear.

Attitudes toward Death: Inherited Taboos

In theory, we know our society ignores or avoids death. What isn't always easy to grasp is the emotional force with which its reality can hit you. Imagine the shock if the same attitude applied to childbirth and you did not discover how babies were born until you found yourself in labor. Though knowledge and preparation in both cases may not make going through the event any easier, at least it would take away some of the shock.

> *If everyone openly accepts the inevitable, with calmness and dignity, then death is much easier to handle.*

We cannot help inheriting these taboos to a degree. But if it is difficult for our society to be open about death, it's often ten times harder for our immediate family! If everyone openly accepts the inevitable, with calmness and dignity, then death is much easier to handle.

This may be possible for some families with strong religious beliefs and loving, mature relationships. For others, getting to that point may involve overthrowing so many family habits that it becomes impossible, as Guy found.

> 𝔄 "I used to long for someone to say something—just one word—that would show they accepted the truth. We all knew what the truth was, but no one would say it. One of the hardest things of all was seeing my mother doing the housework as usual and not seeming to have any time for death."

Guy felt this attitude denied them all something. One of the conclusions he came to was that death must have its place. If there's no communication about death, at least identifying your own position can be useful: You are caught by a social taboo, a victim of an attitude you didn't create.

You may find that pain makes the barriers come down and that you are able to talk more easily within your family.

You can store the knowledge for outside use—later you may be able to find someone with whom to break the taboo. You may find that pain makes the barriers come down and that you are able to talk more easily within your family.

Otherwise, don't force the issue. Sometimes you must accept that it is just too painful to do anything about it within your own family. Frankness, however desirable it may seem, may not be appropriate for now. Challenging the death taboo head-on with a grief-stricken parent may be more than you (or she) can bear.

Your Own Idea of Death

You will probably need to look at theories about death at some point, especially if you have been brought up with a religious belief. Your parent's death will be one of the biggest challenges to your faith that you will ever encounter. Your parent's death is also one life event that faith does address.

Some people abandon religious faith while facing parental death. Before you reach this point, however, you should talk to someone. If your local minister doesn't seem appropriate to talk to, keep in mind that insight into these matters varies from person to person. Someone else might be more suitable.

The hospital chaplain or priest is experienced in dealing with the kind of spiritual experience you are going through. He or she can usually recommend other people to contact according to your needs and religious background.

The phenomenon of people turning to religion after a close death is common. So is wandering away again. At first we need to find meaning, to absorb the implications of the experience, but after we succeed, the mechanics of formal religion may still seem foreign, even if we have caught some of the original spirit.

> ⁋ Anita, a Catholic, had not bothered about religion for many years. After her mother's death, she went back to the church for about a year, but it did not have what she was looking for. She went to individual counseling and later to a grief support group where she found the warmth that she had not found in the church.
>
> She eventually reconciled with the church by taking some of the beliefs but leaving all the ritual. "I don't go to church now, but I do have certain deep beliefs. I suppose most priests' hair would stand on end to hear me say that, but it's simple. I'm comfortable that way. I couldn't go back to church. It's too much like going into the past. I just can't do it."

Whatever you believe, if you haven't had a close experience with death before, chances are your faith and your own ideas of death are inadequate for your present needs. For example, we tend to have a paternalistic view of God in our society (God the Father and sometimes Mary the Mother). The implications of this need further exploration once your own mother or father dies. Both for now and for later, you need to make your own *myth of death*: a private, personal view of death that isn't open to other people's skepticism or rationality.

It isn't really a matter of thinking it through and deciding what you do and don't believe. Your myth doesn't need to have anything to do with literal fact. It's an overall attitude that you achieve quietly, through slow and careful thought, reading and talking.

In other words, you must live through it if the end product is to be worthwhile. This morsel of experience can be one of the most valuable residues of a parent's death. While it can take many years to achieve, the earlier you can come to terms with death in your own way, the better.

To start this process, you may want to examine other people's ideas of death, past and present: the concept of heaven, for example, or the more recent phenomenon of near-death experiences. Looking at other cultures may help.

In ancient Crete, funerals were happy affairs during which the soul, freed from life, was pictured as being released into the blue sky. Without indulging in escapist spiritual fantasies, make your own private myth to help you deal with the reality of death in your life.

Reading can help. There are many books on death and dying in general. The book you choose is personal and it is helpful to be selective, even disciplined. You might find some books too intense, too spiritually speculative, too medically detailed or too dry for your needs.

In addition, there are anthologies of poetry and literature especially chosen for those facing death. You can also turn to the work of individual authors and make choices for yourself. These writings on life experience may be helpful because the authors went through what you are going through now.

8

You and Your Surviving Parent

ONE EFFECT OF LOSING A PARENT is that another person is left behind whose grief is usually seen as worse than yours. It can be difficult to handle selfish grief when comforting your surviving parent, to act parentally and give love and support when you need parenting so much. You may rise to the challenge with newfound maturity.

Some parents and children are drawn closer together by their grief and a strong feeling that outsiders don't really understand. As with the parent who has died, you need to deal with your surviving parent as a person. His or her role has changed drastically. No longer part of a pair with vast, united capacities for remoteness or laughter, anger or serenity, he or she feels like half a person after experiencing one of life's most crushing blows.

> *As with the parent who has died, you need to deal with your surviving parent as a person.*

This is a frightening responsibility if you fear your mother may commit suicide or simply dwindle away and die because she can't bear life without her partner. If you're truly afraid this is a possibility, consult a doctor. Remember you can only do so much. You are *not* responsible for your surviving parent's life.

Even leaving out such extreme fears, you still have to deal with a dramatic change in your relationship. Balance can be difficult to achieve because, although you may feel the need to be supportive, you can't overstep the parent-child boundaries.

You can't suddenly start acting too parentally toward someone who has always been your parent, even though you may need to take on more responsibility for her than ever before. It's a situation that requires a lot of tact because grief leaves people so stunned.

Seeing your surviving parent apparently helpless may tempt you to rush in with formulas to make it better—anything from a new hairdo to moving to another house, apartment or mobile home. You must remember that another person's grief can't be managed or controlled like this. Grief needs to run its course.

Grief needs to run its course.

Trying to distract your surviving parent before it is time just won't work. Also, it can be a sign that you refuse to either accept what has happened or allow your mother to mourn as she needs. It's almost taking advantage of her sorrow to persuade her to take actions she might not have taken otherwise.

> ≈ After Tom died, Michael's brothers shared the expense and sent Michael's mother, Gloria, on a vacation to southern France. Although well-meant, forcing Gloria to go away did little for her grief. When she returned she went to her house and refused to see anyone for a month.

Your surviving parent is probably exhausted, especially if she was involved in prolonged care. She needs time to recover from this exhaustion, the beginning of the grieving process.

Some other surviving parents cling to their roles as fathers or mothers and continue to take care of you, worrying about your feelings instead of coming to terms with their own. This makes it more difficult to do anything for your parent. Later it can be a source of regret that you didn't all go through the death with equally shared emotions.

Different families play at being strong in different ways. A parent or child who has been the leader and decision maker may have trouble admitting that he or she is just as grief-stricken as the rest of the family.

Your surviving parent may feel that he now has a dual role, that his responsibility toward you is doubled and that he needs to be *both* father and mother to you. When your surviving parent babies you this way, worrying about how *you're* taking it instead of how he is, you may be tempted to pretend that life hasn't changed as much as you know it has. Keep a clear head, even under the pressure of dealing with your own emotional needs.

> ⚚ Her father, a gentle person, had not liked Maria nursing her mother, especially when it involved jobs such as helping with colostomy bags. He liked to think of Maria as younger and less resilient than she really was—as a little girl, his little daughter.
>
> Although Maria would have liked to be taken care of, she wasn't convinced that she should allow her father to do that. She felt he was glossing over his own grief in this way, even evading it, and that it deprived them of the chance to mourn together.

In some cases, the death of one parent doesn't make that much difference in the child's relationship with the surviving one. This can happen when parents and children lost touch years back or never really established contact at all. In this case, grief involves mourning for what *never* existed, the deeper relationship with your surviving parent. It may not be possible to change the more superficial contact you have.

How Much Support?

After the death of one parent, your relationship with your surviving parent may become stronger. Outsiders are automatically excluded. Just being there for your parent is probably the best way to offer this intimate support, although it's important to remember that all you can do is offer.

> ⚚ "My mother was the only one who really understood. We didn't want to see anyone else.

We needed to talk about my father. It was natural
for me to stay at home with her until I got married.
I wanted to give her that time; I owed it to her.
The support wasn't a one-way thing. We supported
each other."

Your grieving mother may not be willing or able to accept
support, despite your efforts. The loss of a parent or spouse
touches you to the core and is one of
the most private griefs known. Barging
in emotionally is not the answer.

*Barging in emotionally
is not the answer.*

So, if your surviving parent doesn't
want to talk about it, there isn't much you can do. Silence may be
your mother's best method of survival. All you can do is be ready
to follow up any openings she may give. In the end, we all live
alone with our own grief.

Questions arise during this period about what your role
should be:

- How much support can or should you give?

- What is support anyway?

- Do you have to be a substitute for the lost parent?

- How can you best help your surviving parent?

- Is it arrogant to even try to comfort him after such a loss?

Grief absorbs people to the core, perhaps making them
appear self-centered. Keep this in mind for both you and your
surviving parent during daily events. Let him grieve in his own
way and time.

On the most basic emotional level, it is difficult to accept
that our parents, the gods of our childhood, can fail. Traces of
childhood jealousy or insecurity can also make it hard to accept
that no one can be a substitute for the person who is gone.
However, even if this were possible, it may not be the healthiest
option. People spend their lives looking after a widowed parent,
which can involve the stresses discussed later in chapter 10.

It's also true that getting on with life and caring for another
person may fill the vacuum of those first empty days and weeks.

Just be careful to strike a balance between supporting your parent and expressing your own grief.

This is especially true if your experience isn't drawing you closer to your surviving parent. Research has repeatedly stressed the need to express grief. It isn't healthy to suppress it, to be too confident in your ability to cope. No matter how much you feel you should support your parent, you must acknowledge your own sorrow. Grieve *with* your parent instead of being consciously and cheerfully supportive.

However, many factors can complicate grieving together: your relationship, the ups and downs of grief in your parent, both of your needs for your own space and any feelings you may have that her grief is more important than yours (or vice versa).

With this in mind, the best support you can give is just to be there. Don't try to be the perfect child, don't try to comfort grief away before its time. Accept the ebb and flow of grief in your surviving parent and in yourself.

Twice Bereaved?

What if grief doesn't draw you and your father closer together? Sometimes, it may not be possible to reach your surviving parent, who shuts himself away with his sorrow. This is especially true if the communication in your previous relationship was limited.

> ‿ Guy felt that death had deprived him of both parents. He had to deal not only with the loss of his father, but also with the loss of his grief-stricken mother whom, after two years, he described as still remote. This led to feelings of resentment toward his mother.
>
> Guy had no trouble identifying those feelings as childish and irrational, the feeling that his mother could have done more to prevent his father's death, that somehow she was unconsciously responsible for it. Guy realized that this was his grief talking, not an objective fact about his mother.

The course of relationships in grief will run on the tracks laid down before the death.

The course of relationships in grief will run on the tracks laid down before the death. A restrained relationship with your surviving parent can bring out all the leftover feelings from childhood with full force. This can leave you feeling that your emotions are unimportant or that your grief is merely childish self-pity in comparison with that of your surviving parent.

> ⁂ At times Guy had to suppress his own need to grieve in the face of one who so obviously had the right to be first mourner. If his mother didn't show her feelings, what right had he to show his? This feeling was confirmed by one friend who, when first told the news of Guy's father's death, burst out, "Oh, your poor, poor mother!" Guy didn't doubt this was the right and proper reaction, but where did it leave him?

Allowing your grief to be devalued in this way, feeling that yours is inferior to your remaining parent's (something that can have its roots in low self-esteem) is a humiliating experience that you really don't need. Who is going to measure grief? Unfortunately, this is an example of how a moment's thoughtlessness can grate on the sensitivity of the newly bereaved, creating even more guilt.

It took Guy many years before he could see his friend's comment for what it was: a thoughtless blurting-out of what her feelings would be if she lost her own husband.

In addition, these feelings don't help your surviving parent either. They can leave her even more isolated than she would have been. You cannot place your surviving parent on a pedestal of grief. You are both grieving equally. The grief, however, is not completely shared and you have to respect your surviving parent's need for his own space. It may hurt to be told "You just don't understand," but it certainly doesn't help to measure who is suffering more.

You and your parent are mourning different people, a parent and a spouse. You cannot fully empathize with all the details of someone else's relationship. They shared time, more time than your whole life. They shared life experiences that you may have yet to go through, such as marriage and the birth of children.

Your mother lost the person with whom she lived on a day-to-day, *physical* basis. Research has shown that one of the things missed most when a partner dies is *touch*. Older people especially, who live isolated lives, may go for months or even years without ever being touched after the death of their partner.

Likewise, your surviving parent can't quite enter into what the loss of your father or mother means to you. The loss of security, the power of all those childhood memories, the general farewell to your past are exclusive to you.

Lifestyle Changes

If death leaves your mother alone, you may naturally want to provide company for her, either by moving in with her for a while or by having her come live with you. You should give it time before making this a permanent decision.

In general, people should not make any major decisions until a year or two after a bereavement. Many a widow (or widower) has sold her old house soon after the death, only to regret it later on.

> *In general, people should not make any major decisions until a year or two after a bereavement.*

When grief has lost its first edge, the memories associated with the old place become valuable rather than painful. Also, the old routine and familiarity can help someone live through her grief. So, it might be a good idea for your parent to visit you for a few weeks first, before you make any long-term decision.

However, there's also the possibility that your parent may be left in a house too large or expensive for him or her to manage alone, in which case an early move could be beneficial.

When Stephen's father died, he and his brothers and sisters sold the large old family home to buy their mother a small modern apartment. The family was amazed at how much she enjoyed her new apartment. And, once her initial grief was over, she seemed happier there than she had been for years.

Losing Your Favorite Parent

Mourning is affected by a troubled relationship with the dead parent, but it can also be complicated if you're left with the parent you feel less close to. Grief doesn't always draw people closer together. It can be surprising how persistent old habits of communication or noncommunication are.

> ~C Michael felt his mother always talked on a superficial level with him. This didn't change after Tom's death, and Michael felt cheated of the long talks about Tom they could have had, of the memories she could have shared with him.

In a wider sense, what happens if you lose the family communicator? Often in a family, one parent (often, but not always, the mother) takes on the role of mediator between the different personalities in the house. He or she is the one who clears everyone's path, who forms a bridge between parents and children, who explains motivations and diverts anger, the one who enables family life to run smoothly.

When this parent dies, the family status quo breaks up, either slowly or immediately. During the following period, the family may seem to drift apart, especially if the children are adult and living their own lives. In time, one of the children may find herself taking over this role (or the different siblings will take on different parts of it). He or she becomes the one to remember birthdays, to invite people for Christmas or to visit other family members.

Meanwhile, you're left without the comforting and insulating presence of your dead parent, which can mean facing a real relationship with your surviving parent for the first time. Looking at the long term, this can be an opportunity to build a new relationship with that parent.

With growing maturity, we always tend to appreciate factors of our parents' personalities that we never noticed before. This process is heightened when you're left face to face with one parent. However, you can't expect too much. Maturity also means accepting people, including parents, as they are.

> *Maturity also means accepting people, including parents, as they are.*

Being Left with Your Favorite Parent

≈ Heather, an only child, had some ambivalence in her grief. She'd always been closer to her mother than her father. When her father, Bob, died, she also had to cope with a faint feeling of relief that at least her mother hadn't died. In fact, her mother and she had had a habit of teasing Bob—ganging up on him, as he used to say. Now that he was dead, they were in the position of having to take seriously someone they'd spent a lot of time laughing at.

When you have lost the parent you didn't get along with, the traditional family structure needs a complete reappraisal. Heather, for instance, suddenly realized how a family tradition of joking around had given both her and her mother a kind of safety and had kept her relationship with her father from developing any further.

You may feel guilty if you're at all relieved that at least your favorite parent was spared. This can be connected with jealousy if the surviving parent is grief-stricken by his loss. But this doesn't mean that your grief is any less genuine.

Your Parent's Expectations

It is easy, especially some time after the death, to expect too much of your surviving parent. He should pull himself together, recarpet the ugly hall, dispose of the dead parent's possessions or go ahead and move instead of just talking about it.

If you don't live together and you see him only on visits, such things are likely to be clearer to you than to him. It may be much more difficult for your parent to move on than you realize.

Making a change—any change—is a deep admission that life goes on, an admission he may not be ready to make yet. It can take many months or years before your surviving parent can deal completely with his grief. He may need support, in varying degrees, for being just as he is during that time.

> *To him, it may seem like a betrayal to move ahead with life.*

To him, it may seem like a betrayal to move ahead with life or to admit, once and for all, that death has taken his partner. He knows that time will not bring her back and may think that their shared past would be violated by a change or a move.

However, at some point, you may sense that your parent would like to move on in some way but can't do it alone. Perhaps he would welcome a gentle push. One way of tackling this can be with the help of your brothers and sisters.

> Maria and her sister put their heads together and decided their father, Dick, wouldn't mind if they disposed of all their mother's things. "I would have felt weird coming in by myself and going through the house, but together it was no problem. We just sensed the time was ripe and that's how it turned out. He was definitely relieved when we took matters into our hands."

Maria's comment raises a point worth noting: The signs your parent gives indicate his readiness to move on. These may be just subtle hints or more obvious signs, like a move to sell the old house. But be careful in your judgements: Your father may need to talk about his plans for a while before actually putting them into action. There's a big difference between talking about selling the house and hiring a real-estate agent. You can't do the entire job for him, but you can help out if he shows he's ready to be helped.

Caring for Your Surviving Parent

Apart from emotional support, one of the most immediate ways you can help your remaining parent is on a practical level: making sure she eats, shops and generally takes care of herself. A balance is necessary if you want to avoid becoming intrusive. You have to judge how far to go.

Do you want to move in for a while and look after your parent? Is it a case of weekly visits, during which you check the contents of the refrigerator and cupboards, plus make a trip to the supermarket? Will you make frequent phone calls to keep in touch?

If the dead person was always the one to take care of the daily routine, you might need to help in a variety of areas, such as taking care of the car, paying the mortgage, shopping or balancing the checkbook. But don't try to do too much. Part of your surviving parent's readjustment must be learning to take care of herself.

For now, try to make sure your parent eats properly, keeping her stocked up with fresh fruit and other nutritious food. Bring food when you visit and cook meals for her, if it's appropriate. Buy other basics that your dead parent always took care of, such as new socks, soap, toilet paper, vacuum bags and so on.

Don't bring a lot of alcohol into the house. It isn't a question of your parent becoming dependent on it—even a couple of glasses can make her feel extremely uncomfortable. It can cause her to feel all her emotions more acutely and express her emotions more freely than she really wants to.

Sharing the Care

How you share the care of your surviving parent partly depends on how much family you have and how available they are. A sister with a new baby or a brother who lives several states or a province away won't be able to contribute on the same scale as you if you're unattached and live nearby.

Siblings may also make excuses for not helping more. They may feel too busy, even though it's probably an illusion in many cases. You may need to work out exactly how much help you can give, clearly stating your position to other family members along with a clearly stated request for more involvement on their part.

You also need to remember your parent's own preferences, which can create another occasion for sibling rivalry.

> ◈ Colin was angered that his mother obviously preferred to spend Christmas with his brother. Michael felt his mother could have visited his young children more often. She seemed to spend more time with his oldest brother's family.

If your family is nearby, available and friendly, try to share the care. Do not take everything upon yourself when caring for your surviving parent. The pull toward caring for a bereaved parent is strong. But the pull toward living your own life also needs attention—if not right now, then in the future.

9

Help

THE HELP AND SUPPORT a person receives after a death can also affect the quality of bereavement. Once the initial isolation of grief has passed, you may need to talk about your lost parent and your grief experience.

Perhaps you've already been able to do this within your immediate circle of family or friends. But you also need to make a more objective, deeper appraisal. This might be with people who know neither you nor your family but who have been in the same position of losing a mother or father. These can be people you've met socially or at a grief support group. Or you may need specialized professional help, perhaps no more than a checkup from your doctor for recurrent headaches, perhaps a commitment to some form of therapy for a while.

Choose what you think you need with care and flexibility. Don't hesitate to change if you feel your choice isn't helping. You don't have to stick with a therapist who makes you feel inadequate in your grief just because you hope the therapy may be doing your soul good. Find people who can give genuine support.

Also make sure that your surviving parent knows what help is available, even if he doesn't want to accept it now. There may come a time when a grief support group could help him get back on his feet again. But you can't force this issue. When it comes to seeking help, you must consider your own needs first. In the end, you can only work through *your* grief and you are the best person to help yourself.

Being Ready for Help

The motivation that drives you to ask for help can be complex and delicate. For a while after a death, you may feel strongly that others can't help, or that you shouldn't even be looking for help. Grief can be so all-embracing that, while you may long to break through it, you may be held back because you feel so remote from other people.

They go about their daily concerns with a happy lack of self-consciousness, unaware of how your life has been shaken to its core. You may ask yourself whether it is fair to impose on them, to ask them to *share* your shock and devastation.

But, you can't live for too long with such a strong feeling of being cut off from other people. The fact that it hasn't happened to them *can* keep them from truly feeling for you. It's always easier to protect yourself from others' sorrow than your own.

Try to judge what sort of feedback you're going to get. If a friend is absorbed by a new baby, or an aunt is moving (and if they've never been through grief themselves), they may not be able to give you the in-depth attention you feel you need.

This is when you may need to seek help more actively as well as determine if you are ready for help. You may need to *think* about looking for help for a while before you can actually bring yourself to act. A move toward help is the beginning of a general move ahead. You may simply have more grieving to do before you are ready for that.

How can you become ready? There is no simple answer. You do need to allow yourself enough time to grieve. You also need to be open to the possibility of help as much as possible. Even if you don't want to talk this year, you might be able to next year.

The desire for company on some days may be matched by an equal desire for solitude on others.

Also, your wish for help may come and go. The desire for company on some days may be matched by an equal desire for solitude on others. Your feelings toward others can range from an almost desperate kind of dependence ("I must talk to so-and-so. She's the only one who will understand.") to deep anger or even indifference.

The best way to get through this confusing time is to be gentle with yourself. Don't be too concerned about the shifts in your emotions toward others, and what they may think of you. Friends new and old will be there for you when you are ready for them.

Friends

So, can your existing friends help? Those who still have their parents may not be nearly as supportive as you hope because they just haven't been through your experience. Hearing about it can be a threat to their own security. It hasn't happened to them yet and naturally they don't want it to.

Friends new and old will be there for you when you are ready for them.

Although they may express some sympathy, it is easy for them to retreat into self-defense, to turn away from the subject. Besides, it's hard for them to know what to say or do, although you will always appreciate them making the effort.

> ⁀ℂ Anita was touched when an old friend of hers invited her to go on a week-long hiking tour soon after her mother's death. "She was the only person who tried to do something solid and practical. She gave up a week of her time. That's the sort of thing you never forget."

You are also in danger of draining friends dry or of converting them into substitute parents. This is especially true if you perceive these people as being stronger and better than you. You may idealize them or project onto them fantasies of a kind of security that in reality belongs to parents.

> ⁀ℂ Not wanting to overburden her fiancé with her grief, Maria got into the habit of visiting a couple she knew, a few years older than her, who had no

(Continued . . .)

children of their own. Even at the time, she realized she was painting a rosy picture of them and choosing to ignore their all-too-human characteristics.

But she could not help visualizing them as a haven of security, an environment where quarrels rarely took place or were soothed over with a few wise words. She realized, however, that her constant visits were beginning to put a strain on two busy people. She married and moved away before this became too obvious.

Just after a loss is not a good time to start a friendship. With emotional energy absorbed by grief, it is difficult to take an active, vital part in other relationships. You may envy the normal lives of others. It's tough to accept that they can afford to care about the details of their shopping and work, when your own normality and balance has been so shattered. In the anguish of grief, the sublime can easily merge into the ridiculous, as Maria recounts.

🙼 I found myself trying to copy the details of their lives. I suppose I hoped I could get rid of my uncomfortable feelings and be more like them. I couldn't wait to get married so I'd be happy and settled, too. I wanted to buy a house like theirs. I'd even shop for food in the same store they did!

If friends cannot help you evade grief, an existing friend can be a real godsend if he's been through your experience.

🙼 Michael had one good friend who lost his mother shortly after Michael lost his father. Michael found their talks truly helpful in coming to grips with his feelings.

But, just having gone through the same experience isn't always a guarantee of mutual support.

🙼 In theory, Maria and Anita, having met at the hospital where their mothers died, could have made supportive friends for each other, but Anita envied Maria's engagement and the fact that she was comparatively settled.

Perhaps also they were too similar. Both
certainly sought out older, mother-type women
friends for a while. Also, neither liked to see each
other because it stirred up memories of the hospital.

Then there are the friends who ignore you, half-consciously,
or who avoid contacting you from day to day because they don't
know what to say. In this case, it may be up to you to get in touch
with them. It is hard to have to support uncertain friends with
explanations and reassurance, but hopefully you will only need to
go through this once. After your initial frankness, they may be
ready to show much more understanding than you hoped. Friends
have their limitations and they have their own lives to lead, but try
to be open to help if they offer. It often comes when you least
expect it.

Help from a Minister

Chapter 7 looks at how your ideas about spiritual life and your
attitude toward the church might change after a parent's death.
Now is a time when you might be tempted to seek support and
understanding from one church or another. Yet many barriers can
hold you back from consulting a minister, priest or rabbi for
guidance during this time.

An opposition to religion, doubt and disbelief or years of
neglecting the family religion can all be reasons. The experience
of finally gathering up courage to go and discuss your spiritual
experience with someone can be disappointing, routine or even
slightly funny.

⟫ Anita had been brought up Catholic but had
lapsed in recent years. She began attending a nearby
church. Misled by its aura of incense and the regular
confessions that took place, she believed it to be
Catholic. It wasn't until she found herself face to face
with the priest for a heart-to-heart talk that she
realized it was Episcopalian.

(Continued . . .)

That was an embarrassing meeting during which Anita did her best to get out of the situation without offending him and the elderly minister did his best to show how willing he was to help!

Some people hold back from seeking help because, if they found it, there would be nothing else to look for.

Implicit in this story is the demand that the help be of the right kind. Some people hold back from seeking help because, if they found it, there would be nothing else to look for.

Perhaps you fear that a reassuring chat with someone seen as possessing superior spiritual knowledge would be a bit of a letdown. It would interrupt the spiritual quest that can be part of the painful privilege of grief. Colin didn't want to be handed answers on a plate.

> ≥€ "I didn't want my grieving methodically arranged by a man of religion. There were too many loose ends. Besides, it would have deprived me of the chance to go through it alone. More than that, I felt it was something I was *meant* to go through alone."

Ministers, priests and rabbis have just as many doubts and fears as laypeople, if not more. They might even argue that a confused struggle with doubt is nearer to spiritual clarity than unquestioning complacence. Certainly, an experienced rabbi might be able to point out how this inner turmoil, this ruthless sorting through of old ideas, can eventually lead to new, stronger ideas. By sharing your feelings honestly, you could help them develop fresh insights into the deepest questions about life and death, which are the bedrock of their existence.

Ministers, priests and rabbis are there to deal with the questions that may be haunting you. Is there life after death and if so what kind? Are the dead aware of us? Why did my mother or father have to die just then, in that way? What, if anything, is the value of pain and of unanswered prayers? Even if ministers don't have all the answers, they too may count it as a painful privilege to share your grief for a time.

Using Your Doctor

Grief drains your energy and leaves you more vulnerable to illness and hypochondria. Although grief itself is not an illness, it is a very real experience that takes a lot of effort to live through. Bereaved people become ill more often, especially during the first year.

The links between body and mind are real.

But the subtle links between mind and body should not mean that you become ashamed of imaginary illnesses. Your resistance to infection is lowered because of the stress of grieving. The links between body and mind are real.

Sometimes people develop illnesses that mimic the illnesses the dead parent died from. Chapter 5 includes the story of Heather, who developed stomach and bowel problems with similar and alarming symptoms to those of her father's disease.

In the first year or so following your bereavement, you may go to the doctor more often for assorted physical ailments and perhaps also for help with your grief-associated emotions. Depending on personality and experience, your doctor may be able to direct you to some counseling if you feel you need it. Depending on your insurance plan, you may not need a referral to see a psychologist or other mental health professional.

You may want to talk over your parent's illness and death with the doctor, to get details straight that you were too confused to understand at the time. Could it have been diagnosed earlier? Was it treated properly? Answers to such questions can not only reassure you and clear your mind, they can also be important in determining your own future health.

For example, if your mother died of breast cancer, you'll want to pay closer attention to self-testing and screening. If your father died of heart disease, you will probably benefit from checking and modifying your own eating and exercise habits.

Trusting your doctor is a major factor in how you use him or her during this time. This may be more difficult if your doctor is the same person who treated your parent. Even if you don't like your doctor, consider the advantages of him or her knowing your family history against the possible advantages of a new, more understanding physician.

No matter how sympathetic your doctor may be, don't forget that he or she is pressed for time. So have a list ready, in case you forget something, and be sure to mention your chief concern first.

It can be all too easy, when face to face with the doctor, to be frightened and forget your worry that the pain in your chest is your heart about to fail. If you don't come out and say what you're worried about, you might make several more visits with other symptoms that cover up your chief anxiety.

No matter how silly you may feel talking about your fears, your doctor has heard worse. Besides, giving reassurance is a valid part of a doctor's job, not just because doctors do a lot of it, but because worry *can* make you sick.

If you are sick, don't assume you are just suffering from grief or that it is all in your mind. If necessary, ask for another visit or a second opinion. Make sure you are getting all the medical attention you need.

Taking Care of Yourself

You need to maintain the same level of care for yourself that you spent (or would have liked to have spent) on your parent when he was dying. This can be hard to do after a death, when it's all too easy to feel that everyone dies, so why bother? You will feel better if you take care of yourself right now. Do this for the sake of others if you can't yet bring yourself to do it for your own sake.

Whatever your situation, be aware of your own value.

Do it for the sake of your surviving parent, for your friends or for your own family.

Whatever your situation, be aware of your own value. Don't let grief drive you into the ground. The extent to which you care for yourself partly depends on your existing self-esteem and partly on how good your emotional security has been in the past. It is more of an effort for some people than for others.

If you're out of the habit of taking care of yourself, treat yourself as you would a special guest. Neatness and cleanliness (or the opposite) are well known for their effects on morale. So make your surroundings as appealing as possible, even if you live alone. You may not have the energy for redecorating, but keeping your house clean, making yourself something special for dinner and having fresh flowers around are little things that can help you move ahead.

Spending money on yourself can also bring a valuable feeling of release. It doesn't have to be large amounts: a new pillow or pair of slippers, a haircut, some attractive stationery, anything that makes you feel more taken care of. Hoarding money can be a symptom of hoarding life, of being afraid to move ahead because the death experience has intimidated you. So try to spend money freely sometimes.

Also, it can be easy to ignore the broken TV or the worn towels that you've been living with for months. Look around and find other

> *Spending money on yourself can also bring a valuable feeling of release.*

little ways to take care of yourself and fix up your surroundings.

At some point, when you feel stronger, you may want to catch up on taking care of your house or apartment, beyond basic housekeeping. But don't rush into big, time-consuming projects unless you are sure that grief is no longer depleting so much of your energy.

The importance of eating and resting well must be stressed again. Try not to indulge in too many comfort habits, such as eating chocolate, which is easy to slip into at such a time. Or if you do, at least make sure you eat a well-balanced meal first. Make the effort to cook for yourself, even though not liking food can be a part of grief.

> ⌘ Everything Heather ate tasted like cotton. She lost twelve pounds in the months after her father's death. A friend suggested she eat small healthy meals: fresh fruit and vegetables; lowfat protein (chicken or fish); brown rice and whole-wheat bread. This helped her regain her health and her appetite.

Grief can intensify addictive habits, such as drinking too much alcohol. This is especially true if you had a dependent relationship with your dead parent or a well-established drinking habit before the loss, or both. The danger to your health from both heavy drinking and smoking can keep you from resuming good eating habits and can cause further health problems. Recognizing this fact is one thing. Battling against a well-established habit or an addiction is quite another. Recognizing when you need help is vital, so if you feel you can't do it alone, don't be ashamed to ask for help.

Grief Support Groups

A number of bereavement organizations exist throughout North America. Bereavement counselors report that more people are coming to talk about the death of a mother or father than used to be the case. You may need to look at more than one organization before finding one that you like.

Don't give up if you try one, find it unsympathetic and decide it isn't for you. Another group may have a slightly different format or people you feel more at ease with.

While bereavement is a great equalizer, it makes sense to look for a group you feel at home with. Some people need only one or two visits, just to know they are not weird and that their soaring emotions are normal.

The Useful Addresses section of this book gives the headquarters of national support organizations. You may also be able to find more information from your doctor, minister, the library or on the Internet. The grief support group will put you in touch either with other people who have had your experience or with a counselor specifically trained to deal with the complications of mourning.

Sometimes, it can be difficult to untangle grief from a range of other emotions or life problems. In this case you may also want to go to a group that deals specifically with your problem. If one doesn't exist, why not start one yourself?

This doesn't mean you have to meet with a group for the rest of your life. Use it at your discretion and don't hesitate to do something else when you feel ready. The ultimate goal of going to any group is to discover the sources of inner strength that enable you to move toward true adult independence. Some people also find satisfaction in eventually contributing to such groups as a leader or organizer of some kind, or as a helper or trained counselor.

On the other hand, you may need to talk with a counselor or psychologist to untangle those aspects of your life that are giving you trouble, to look at yourself in greater depth. Start by looking for someone who is trained in bereavement, someone familiar with the nature and pace of grief. If your needs go beyond those of bereavement, you may need a psychiatrist.

Reviewing What Has Happened

Some people feel the urge to write down what has happened to them, especially if their parent died a harrowing or violent death. This can be a way of making sense of the event, of finding order in what otherwise appears to be random suffering.

> In her early twenties, Clare nursed both parents through cancer and saw them die within weeks of each other. About eighteen months after their deaths, she began to write a novel about her experience. It all came out. While she eventually realized she couldn't publish it, she was certain that writing such a painful testimony was a valuable effort.

This kind of writing can be helpful in attempting to put the death in its place in your life, but it demands perseverance. It is also the kind of project that seems more intimidating beforehand than afterward. Although it may cost you some pain, the end result can be new strength that comes from purging your memory. Another bonus is increased self-knowledge.

While writing, Clare found that along with her unselfish act of nursing her parents, she experienced many bitter feelings. "It

You may not be able to look at your parent's illness and death in isolation.

wasn't all a warm glow of satisfaction that I was doing the right thing." She had to come to terms with many unsatisfactory elements in her relationship with both parents. In other words, she wasn't just writing the history of the illness, but the history of all their lives.

You may not be able to look at your parent's illness and death in isolation. You may have to look at how family relationships have contributed to the way you are and aspects of your life and character you feel guilty or unhappy about.

Getting these down in black and white can help clear the ground for new growth. Know your own strength before you embark on this—not too soon after the death, when you still may be too hurt to handle such material.

The purpose of such a project is *not* to be hard on yourself. Don't worry about it being a work of art. Try starting in note form on index cards, piece by piece as you feel like it. It's also a good idea to work on a physical project at the same time, such as doing yardwork or washing the car.

Not only do you need physical work to counteract your mental work, memories do come to you while you're absorbed in manual work. We tend to block out unpleasant details, even if we believe we'll never forget at the time. After you start writing, it may be weeks before all the memories drift back.

In Memorial

One of the strongest needs after the death of a parent is to keep in touch somehow with the person who has died. This can be very helpful in determining the course of your grief. Some people feel that caring for their parent's grave is a chance to do a last service for their dead parent.

It seems to smooth over any last little misunderstandings and makes good any past defects in attention. For some, it's simply an act of respect for their memory, a reassurance that someone who was once so important will not be forgotten. Go to any cemetery on the weekend and you will see people carrying flowers, watering cans, trowels and new plants to the graves of their loved ones.

This can be a time when you begin to understand the value of traditional ways of paying respect to the dead—from taking care of the grave to lighting candles or arranging for requiem masses to be said. However, these channels may not seem right for you. You may want to do more, to make your own personal contribution to your parent's memory, or to do so with another family member.

> ✧ Michael planted a tree at his father's graveside and visited regularly to take care of it, sometimes on his own and sometimes with a brother. Heather, whose father died of cancer, made an annual contribution to a cancer-research charity in his memory. She also met her mother at the grave once a month, to tend it or just to stand there for a few minutes.

Other Family Members

Other family members can be a great source of help when it comes to the long-term appraisal of grief and your relationship with dead parents.

> ✧ Maria and her grandmother had always been close because when Maria's mother had gone back to work, her grandmother had helped raise her. She was able to share all the knowledge of Maria's mother and of Maria's early years, and so she was a great source of consolation.

> ✧ Two of Guy's second cousins visited from Australia. Guy found it was satisfying to see their family resemblance to his father and to feel that they'd come partly to pay tribute to his memory.

Sometime during your grief, you may long for people to talk with about your dead father or mother—people who knew them well. Family members are often the nearest source of information, even if you sometimes have to work diligently to distinguish between reality and family myth.

What Doesn't Help

In the tenderness of early bereavement, you are more vulnerable to stray comments from other people, whether negative or positive. While it helps to be aware of this increased sensitivity, you should also be able to trust your instincts in sorting them out. Decide for yourself what is not helpful to protect yourself from any negativity.

Perhaps the most demoralizing attitude is that which preaches the stiff upper lip, which seems to accuse the grieving person of self-pity and moral weakness. It's an attitude that advises you to pull yourself together and get on with it because plenty of other people in the world are worse off than you. This view ignores the quality of your grief to focus on false estimates of quantity.

Just as bad, if more sickening, is the view that everything happens for the best and that God has a plan for your life that you will be able to appreciate later. This is a kind of sentimental, oversimplified view of the much tougher fact that a parent's death pulls you forward unexpectedly into new growth.

Be very cautious about seeking consolation in two potentially harmful areas. One is spiritualism (seances or other means) that promise to get in touch with the dead. Apart from anything else, this can be psychologically negative, turning the clock backward in the grieving process. Whether you can see it or not, time does move slowly ahead to the point when you can begin life anew.

The second area is that of new, alternative religions or cults. Beware of those that offer instant answers or demand that you give money or leave home to move in with other members. It is up to you to decide on the type and quality of help you accept, and when you choose to accept it.

10

Starting to Live Again

GRIEF MUST NOT BECOME AN ESCAPE from life. Impossible though it may seem in the shocking beginning, people sometimes slip into a pattern of holding on to grief. Some feel an unspoken fear of going on with life because it brings them closer to the point at which their own parent died. Fear of death leads to fear of life.

At some point you have to start living again. Maybe your marriage is waiting or you've postponed your education to be with the bereaved parent. Perhaps you put on hold your plans for moving to a new house. Whatever it is, you must tackle it, especially if grief is becoming an excuse for not moving ahead with your life.

> *Fear of death leads to fear of life.*

Sometimes it isn't that easy. You *know* the next step and you want to take it, but you linger where you are, comfortable in that position. You put off the next move until you are forced to make it. We can easily acquire habits in grief, just as in other life situations: habits of staying in and not socializing, habits of rushing to be with our surviving parent or of talking only to the same few people. After a while, there can be safety in unhappiness. It can be painful to leave the familiar behind—even familiar pain.

You know when an old mode of living starts to get stale. You feel bored and restless and your mind starts making plans almost independently. Sometimes the date for moving ahead is set for you: a new job to go to, for example, or the birth of a baby. It is harder when you don't feel that inner urge to move ahead, when motivation is lacking or you can't seem to establish any goals.

You also must consider your surviving parent as you plan for the future:

- How closely should your lives be interlinked?
- How much responsibility should you accept for her well-being?
- When do you need to be selfish?
- How can you find a compromise between family and your own personal needs?

Sometimes we only begin to think of ourselves after a parent's death. Perhaps for the first time we have to define an identity independently from our family. If this process is long or convoluted, the result can be an increased, enduring inner strength.

When to Start Again?

It can take years to work through a parent's death, years before you feel your life is back on course. Try to avoid thinking this time is meaningless or a waste, however troubled and bleak it may be.

How quickly you become interested in your future partly depends on which stage of your life you were in when your parent died. If he died while you were at an early or difficult stage, when your plans or identity may have been shaky, it may take longer.

> ∂ℂ Guy's father died when Guy was twenty-one, at a time of transition in his life. He was finishing his studies without definite plans for the future. This lack of clarification was amplified by Guy's own lack of self-confidence and subconscious reliance on his father to point him in the right direction after graduating from college. Until he reached his early thirties, Guy never really felt settled in life.

This can happen to anyone. The twenties are traditionally a time to experiment and seek your identity. Guy's story also shows that your own character and outlook are important factors in how long it takes to find your way after a parent's death. Someone with strong career-path ideas might have had more of an anchor in life.

You also need to differentiate between completely working through the implications of a parent's death (something that sometimes is never finished) and coming through the worst of grief. Although this may take place over a two-year period, grief may also lighten after six months or a year.

Even if you still have a lot of grieving to do, the first impact of sorrow may melt away enough for you to feel you can move ahead with your life.

Getting Stuck in Grief

What if you feel you can't move ahead? If you've been at a certain stage of grief for a long time, you may not be able to see when it's going to end. It is possible to become stuck in grief—to go through life *What if you feel you can't move ahead?* in a kind of settled depression. It's possible to be so intimidated by the death that you no longer have the confidence or will to make plans or enjoy anything.

Be gentle on yourself and lower your expectations. Don't feel that you should put the event behind you or that you should have recovered by now. Grief sometimes just takes more time than you expect. If your grief has not decreased significantly after two years, get some outside help if you have not already done so (see chapter 9).

Prolonged grief can be part of other personality or life difficulties. Sometimes it's hard to disentangle grief from these. The consequences of your parent's death may have unleashed life situations that bring about a bunch of other emotions. Maybe your life slowed down or your plans changed after your parent's death.

It's difficult to separate grief from other sources of misery, such as loneliness, longing for a partner or not liking your job. This is where help comes in. Outside feedback can help you identify more accurately all the aspects of your life you aren't happy with. This may spur you into taking steps to change these feelings.

Another source of pain can be when your surviving parent does not progress in grief or when your sorrow does not keep pace with his. Normally you have more of a life to lead, more to do and more to accomplish. You may need to distinguish between the grief of others and your own grief if the time comes when you feel that it's healthier for you to move on. You also need to distinguish between your opinion of your parent's grief and its real nature. Guilt at wanting to move ahead could lead you to exaggerate grief.

Letting Your Surviving Parent Go

Naturally, your surviving parent is going to be a prime consideration when you think about getting on with your life. But does he or she really depend on you as much as you think? Or is it your own sense of responsibility and perhaps guilt that makes you reluctant to move ahead? This can be particularly strong if you're single and not yet planning on buying your own home.

> ឱ Guy, who was about to start sharing an apartment when his father died, stayed home with his mother and postponed his life for two years. He thought starting any new relationship at that time would be selfish and he was more concerned with his mother's needs than his own needs. If he changed jobs, as he wanted to, and perhaps had to move, it would be too hard on his mother.
>
> In the end, a new job and a girl appeared at about the same time, just as Guy was getting thoroughly depressed with his supportive role. He moved with his girlfriend to another town and, to his surprise, his mother got along just fine.

Letting your life revolve around your parent, perhaps even being a substitute partner, isn't much fun, even though you have the satisfaction of knowing you've done your duty. If you continue this role for too long, it can become a way of hiding from life. Sometimes it may not be much fun for your parent, either. The last thing your parent may want is a sympathetic adult child hanging around if he or she is trying to start a new relationship!

> ᴈ Guy's mother was relieved when he left because she then felt free to do what she wanted. She knew she'd been holding Guy back and that this wasn't right. She was also beginning to feel a need for her own space and freedom. She built a good social life after he left and eventually remarried.

If one parent dies relatively young, as Guy's father did at forty-seven, remarriage is more of a possibility. But even if this isn't likely or never happens, your parent needs to be free to rearrange his or her own life, to rebuild a daily routine. Grief is a *relearning process*: Your surviving parent has to acquire many new habits if he is living alone. Fixing meals, shopping, planning vacations and making new friends are just a few examples.

If you already have a partner or family of your own, the situation is different. You also have to consider how much your surviving parent should be involved in your future plans. Would it be healthier to have more of a break, or could you handle closer contact? After some time has gone by, you may want to reexamine whether you should all live together or if you could create a room in your home for your parent if circumstances permit.

> ᴈ Maria and her husband, John, got into the habit of having her father over for lunch every Sunday. Maria would also drop in once or twice a week to take him food and do some ironing or cleaning. This was fine for about eighteen months, but then Maria and John wanted to start a family. This meant moving to a larger house in a rural area. However, they had qualms about how Maria's father would manage.

(Continued . . .)

They felt he had become dependent on them and that perhaps it had been a mistake to do so much for him. Maria didn't discuss it until she became pregnant and then she explained how she felt about the situation. She and John decided they could manage if her father chose to live with them.

He refused, saying they needed to live their own lives, and that it was time he made more of an effort for himself.

Though tinged with sadness, this decision relieved everyone. Maria's father, having had more experience with new babies than Maria, was being realistic. Maria came to appreciate this when she finally had her own child! You must seek a balance between your own needs and those of your surviving parent, although this balance will never be perfect.

You must seek a balance between your own needs and those of your surviving parent, although this balance will never be perfect.

If you decide to move, you may feel lingering guilt about "abandoning" your surviving parent. As Maria's father knew instinctively, such a move is healthy because it forces the surviving parent to face life more actively.

It may seem natural to arrange for your parent to live with you. This could be the case if your home has extra space or includes separate living quarters.

᷿ Sara made a different decision when her father died. She invited her mother to move in. Sara owned a large country home with adjacent stables. Her mother occupied her own apartment within the house. She had what amounted to a job, helping Sara with her three children, shopping and helping with the girls who came for riding lessons. This arrangement pleased everyone.

Your Elderly Parent

The question of your elderly parent is bigger the older you are. What is the best way of ensuring care for an older parent who may no longer be able to care for himself? The full implications of this question are far-reaching.

As a starting point, consider your parent's personality and his lifestyle. How much help are you willing and able to give toward that lifestyle?

For example, if your father is independent and would hate a rest home or an elder-care apartment, are you willing to drop in when needed? Would it be better to delegate some of the responsibility? How much help will your local social services be able to give? Will your aging parent need nursing? Can you deal with the forgetfulness and hostility associated with conditions such as dementia, senility or Alzheimer's?

As with a dying parent, the care you offer depends on how much he or she is willing to accept.

Last, but by no means least, is your parent's attitude. As with a dying parent, the care you offer depends on how much he or she is willing to accept. It is possible to reach acceptable compromises.

> ⟡ Philip, seventy-nine, had always relished standing on his own two feet, but age had slowed him down. While he was not a danger to himself, he could only move around slowly and had to use a wheelchair for any shopping.
>
> He moved to a complex of one-bedroom apartments equipped for older people, with alarms in case of trouble. This was just a few miles away from his daughter, Rebecca, who visited three times a week. A helper stopped by on the other days.

In this case, both parties felt they needed to keep their distance to maintain some privacy and independence. But what about those who find the call to duty more compelling, who feel that only living with a parent will work? This situation has its dangers.

Disguised dependency

The old maid who stays at home to take care of her aging parents isn't just a cliché of recent history. Though less common today, it still happens, and the loss of parents you've spent years taking care of can provoke a unique reaction.

> ⁂ Jean never left home. She stayed home to care for her father during his last illness and then had to take care of her mother after her father died. She became an angry middle-aged spinster when her mother died. Jean felt that not only was there no one to do the same for her, but in spite of their apparent dependence, her parents had always run her life and were continuing to do so, even though dead.

The days are gone when it was taken for granted that women gave up marriage and a career for aging parents. With these changed expectations, a bitter legacy is often left behind after the death of parents you've spent years taking care of.

You may feel frustrated and lonely, as if you've wasted your life in useless sacrifice. It is harder to start over with the habit of many years of care behind you. You may need extra help to deal with the many negative feelings that such a situation can produce.

> ⁂ Jean started going to a grief support group. She also had intensive counseling for two years in which she was able to rebuild a sense of her own value.

Jean's story illustrates why it is so important to move ahead and not become stuck in a situation that can take years of your life and that you later regret. Your attitudes about your parents don't have to be at either extreme, as Jean points out.

> ⁂ "I was too black and white, too either/or. I thought, either I'm heartless, if I leave them and go off and live my own life, or I'm selfless, loving and doing the right thing if I stay at home. There were just those two alternatives and nothing else, for years. It never occurred to me to get a little

apartment nearby, so I'd have my own space but still
be able to drop in and see them every day.

"Or even just to go out twice a week. I could
have met someone that way, married, and still taken
care of them. I didn't think of it. It just seemed like
they needed me and that was that. Going to a group
and talking to people has expanded my ideas—after
the event, unfortunately."

In other words, compromise may involve pain on one side or
another, but this can be secondary to the deeper needs that urge a
person on into a normal life.

This isn't to condemn all living-together arrangements. There
is a vast difference between a carefully considered invitation to a
parent to move in with you and simply never leaving the nest. As
the box below illustrates, you must consider both practical and
emotional questions when deciding if a parent should move in
with you.

Ask These Questions before Asking a Parent to Move In

- Does your parent need a downstairs room to avoid stairs?
- Will your own children's needs clash with his?
- Will your spouse's needs clash with his?
- Is your parent going to contribute rent or help pay for
  the household expenses? Or will you have to budget for
  extra food, electricity and laundry?
- Will you need to provide transportation? If so, how often?
- How much nursing does your parent need? How much
  might he need in the future?

It is important to agree on all such points beforehand to make sure
you understand the full extent to which you're committing yourself.
Write down the points of the agreement and have you, your spouse
and your parent sign it for future reference in case the original
agreements are overlooked or forgotten.

Leaving the Nest Again: Goals

Do not deny yourself the release of emotional energy that comes from moving ahead. To mature, you need to leave living parents behind to some extent. Bereavement is a great confidence-shaker, so you may have to make a special effort to regain any confidence you have lost.

Do not deny yourself the release of emotional energy that comes from moving ahead.

Setting goals can help restructure a life devastated by grief, as long as you feel ready to move ahead. Goal setting is an important process because it involves a change in thinking patterns that is as profound as the change brought on by grief.

From considering endings, you now have to consider beginnings again. The structure in which happy planning was possible is destroyed. You need to build a new structure before you can plan again, but setting goals now helps prepare you for the future. Achieving small goals will help you move toward bigger decisions and achievements.

> ⚭ Heather started hunting for a new job by having her hair done. Michael approached moving to another house bit by bit, a project that had seemed overwhelming before he started it.

Approach this one day at a time. Don't worry yourself by thinking about all the future possibilities. Don't try to visualize the end result. Just do what you can to bring yourself one small step closer to your goal. Don't forget that your goal can be as simple as living peacefully on a daily basis.

Nonetheless, what about those important long-term goals? Because the fact of death may have reversed your plans for living, it can be difficult to get in touch with your real aims in life again. You may feel you simply can't think of anything you'd really like to achieve. It could be that you've forgotten, that sorrow has driven all dreams from your mind.

One method of getting back in touch with your inner goals is by meditating or daydreaming, allowing your mind to wander through all the possibilities. Give yourself permission to consider the wild, the fantastic and the impossible. You never know, it might just become fact when you decide to focus your energy in that direction!

Circumstances can change quickly, leaving you to face the real possibility of obtaining what was only a vague dream for many years. You don't have to limit your goal to a simple material gain. It can be anything you wish.

> ⤳ Michael always wanted to start his own business but felt tied to his job. This goal seemed more hopeless after his father's death, when he barely had the motivation to crawl through his present job. A year or so after Tom's death, Michael was laid off and a severance payment gave him just enough capital to allow him to start a business.

> ⤳ Guy desperately wanted to buy his own condominium. A simple enough goal, but full of complications. He felt his mother still needed him and his grief was stagnating. In his case, moving toward his goal became possible on the day he realized there was nothing to stop him.

The problem isn't really a matter of what is possible or impossible. The problem lies in making a dream a reality while facing up to the disappointment of losing that dream as something you had wished for. Making your dream into a reality in itself entails loss.

Making your dream into a reality in itself entails loss.

However gradually or quickly you choose to move ahead, the depth of thinking remains the same. The decision to change, to go on living, is profound. In many ways this decision creates itself over a period of time, although you can help it along. Just take care of yourself and use whatever support is available.

Although the decision to move on may grow slowly beneath the surface, with many months of inner preparation, it can sometimes come about suddenly. Some people operate by taking a flying leap into the future, even though this may not end all of their problems completely.

Anita, who spent several months at home, thought at first that her presence had some value for her father. But she soon felt she was just hanging around. She wanted to go to India where she had traveled extensively a few years ago, but she simply couldn't break the pattern of work and home.

"More than that, I couldn't seem to remember or imagine any other life. It was as if all the color had faded from my memories. I suppose it was a kind of depression."

When she recognized everything was "going gray" in her life, she decided she had nothing to lose and left. Once gone, she regretted that she hadn't done it sooner, saving herself months of bleak indecision.

Of course, you have to distinguish between the genuine need to move ahead and the temptation to escape.

Of course, you have to distinguish between the genuine need to move ahead and the temptation to escape. Such a move doesn't have to mean running away from necessary pain.

Anita found there were still painful days when she spent hours crying. The release and stimulus of going away actually helped her get more in touch with her grief. "I liked being alone in a foreign country. I felt more free from restraint. Whether that was good or bad, I don't know. I felt more alive, that I could handle grief better. Before, the dullness of the life I'd been leading had prevented me from feeling anything at all."

This shows how people sometimes need to create their own circumstances in which to come to terms with grief. It may not solve everything, however. You may have to face residual problems when you come home, but weaving your own protection can give you strength until you have to face the reality of the situation on home ground once more.

Lifting of Grief

It could be that Anita, who left two years after her mother's death, was experiencing a *lifting of grief*. This occurs when the main body of sorrow isn't as dark and overwhelming, but the pain can and does return at intervals. Other life events can trigger this lifting of grief, too.

> ❧ Michael and his wife had a third child almost two years after his father's death. This was more than an ordinarily emotional event for Michael, but his regret that his father wasn't there to see his new grandchild was softened by a new acceptance of what had happened.

A death is said to be one of the most common reasons for a pregnancy, an urge to defeat death by bringing a new life into the world.

Grief can leave more unobtrusively. For Maria, it went away little by little under the pressure of everyday business like shopping, cooking and preparing for a baby. One morning she woke up and realized she hadn't thought about her mother for a couple of weeks.

Some people worry that this constitutes a kind of disloyalty to their mother or father. Michael was especially concerned about how impossible it was to hang on to the purity of any emotion and how soon it was run over by ordinary life. He realized that to try to hang on to grief would have been less natural than this forgetting. It was possible to honor his father's memory without the anguish of grief.

> ❧ "In the beginning, I'd break down and cry. My mother would say, 'Time, give it time,' and I'd say, 'No, no, you don't understand.' Now, three years later, I can drive past my father's old house without really noticing it. And I feel sorry in a way, losing that grief."

This brings us to the final point to consider when it comes to restarting your life: the old adage that *time heals*, despite how unbelievable this seems in the beginning. The force of life does move you along. Like it or not, every second new thoughts and impressions come, causing you to move ever further away from your original overwhelming grief. Part of the value of grieving completely is how much more bearable, even comfortable, your feelings become once you've lived through your sorrow.

As Michael pointed out, the lifting of grief is another kind of loss. You lose touch with the emotions that were such a powerful link with your dead mother or father. At this point you begin to realize the value of your experience in grief as a painful tribute paid to love.

11

Toward Maturity: What They Didn't Live to See

ONCE YOUR MAIN GRIEVING IS OVER, you can enter a new phase of living. This can often be a buoyant time, as if held back from life by grief for so long, you rush to meet it with increased vigor. New hopes and prospects seem more precious, perhaps because of the darker experience you've been through. You may have learned to value life more and to be more wholehearted about living in the present. The past takes on the qualities of a dream.

> Sometimes, even years later, the old sorrow will build up unexpectedly.

You never really know how much grieving you have to do. Sometimes, even years later, the old sorrow will build up unexpectedly. It can happen when you are visiting a patient and are hit by that hospital smell, or seeing a friend go through an illness similar to that of your mother's. When a motherly or fatherly friend gives you a hug or you see a family member who resembles your lost parent and who has aged in a way your parent never will, the pain of your loss may return.

Christmas, Hanukkah, other holidays, birthdays and anniversaries can trigger grief. The trigger may be something obvious, such as coming across photos of the past, or it could simply be memories briefly becoming stronger when you're tired or under stress.

Life events such as marriage, the birth of children, illness or another bereavement are times when you may miss your parent in a special way. These are times when you would appreciate the extra loving attention of a mother or father to help you through; times when you simply want to be cared for; times when you long for the kind of talk you can have only with a mother or father.

And there are times when you need someone who knows you best to help you make difficult choices or to reassure you that it will all be okay (that you're loved unconditionally). Such longings may be only fleeting, or they may involve a reawakening of grief that you must live through in your new life situations.

You may tend to paint an ideal picture of the wisdom and tenderness of a parent when remembering. It's easy to forget that parents have human tendencies to misunderstand or give you bad advice!

Even when your grief is a shadow of its former self, the occasional feeling of sadness that your parents aren't there, that they missed out, still hangs on. You could feel they were cheated not just of their own lives, but of the fruits of those other lives— seeing your progress, their grandchildren's progress.

Even later in life, after years have passed, not having your parent around to see you achieve your life goals creates a sense of a missing dimension. The enthusiastic audience isn't there to applaud.

It isn't that you feel incomplete. There is no reason why parental death should prevent you from living as full a life as possible. But you may simply think, "They would have been so happy to see this."

You may sometimes regret your parents' absence without really wanting their presence.

However, you wouldn't want them to come back and see it. Once you have lived through your grief and some time has passed—three, five or ten years— you may sometimes regret your parents' absence without really *wanting* their presence. Too much has happened and you are a different person now, partially because of their death. To turn the clock back is both impossible and psychologically unhealthy.

Also, being without one or both parents means increased personal independence. You are freer from family complications that so often keep people tied to old ways, in spite of their inner urge to move ahead.

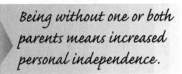

Being without one or both parents means increased personal independence.

After her father had been so ill, Julia was tied to her family more than ever before. She was used to having both parents over for lunch every Saturday, having to be there at Christmas, making sure the children saw their grandparents regularly, until her father died four years later and her mother went to live with her sister. During this time, Julia's plans stood still—she had worked in Canada and married a Canadian who now wanted them to live in Canada.

He felt that Julia, in spite of her apparent independence, was in reality shackled to the bosom of her family, that she wouldn't be truly free to move on until both parents died.

Living parents don't always hold you back. Likewise, their death doesn't always mean instant adult autonomy for you. Whether your family is alive or dead, personal freedom is also a matter of self-knowledge, something that may come with difficulty.

It's a question of how consciously you make your choices: Did you choose to stay near home out of thoughtful concern for aging parents? Or were you drawn back, without really thinking, by some unconscious need for security? Either way, a parent's death forces you to reexamine your position within your family and to redefine your freedom in ways you've never thought of before.

With your parent's death behind you, you must consider the ending of the relationship as you move toward increasing maturity. A parent's death leaves you less able to appreciate him or her as another adult, instead of the parental figure of childhood. While your understanding of them may grow, it isn't the same as being able to verify that understanding with a living person. As we assume more and more adult responsibilities, we take on more and more capacity for understanding.

We can never be sure how well we really knew our parents.

"Now that I have debts of my own, I can appreciate your money worries." "When we lived in that apartment, did you lose your temper with us as children because there was no backyard?" "What was it like for you when Dad was laid off from his job?" are the kinds of questions you may ponder. Many other questions never occur to us until later in life and they can only be answered by speculation. We can never be sure how well we really knew our parents.

Life and Personality Changes

After several years, you usually change substantially in status as well as in character. You may move in with a partner, move ahead in a career or change where you live. You change in ways you never dreamed of in your earlier years.

Sometimes, when you think of your dead parent, it can be hard to reconcile your present self with the person you were at the time of their death. You feel you've changed so much that you might be a stranger to them.

> Jackie, who lost both parents, inherited property and money from them and wasn't interested in a career. She did volunteer work until she married and then quit to have a family. She led a comfortable, stable and happy life. Nevertheless, at each life event—her marriage, the births of her three children—she had to come to terms with the fact that her parents weren't there.
>
> Though sad, she had to admit that this feeling of being alone in the world (in terms of parents) was something of a relief. Parental guidance has advantages and disadvantages! Also, she felt that she was no longer the person she had been at their death, that she was different from the daughter her parents had known.

Much as she might still long to see them, she couldn't help wondering if they'd have much to say to each other anymore, because her parents had missed so many of her most important life events.

This happens to some extent when your parents are alive. You form your own life and identity. Losing touch, though painful at times, is exactly what enables you to form your new life. Jackie's story illustrates a healthy reluctance to go back in time or to hold on to old feelings and old identities.

Even when time and experience have made you into someone different from the person your parents knew, it is possible to feel that they are still with you at some level. You carry their essence with you throughout life, even when some of the memories have faded.

You carry their essence with you throughout life, even when some of the memories have faded.

Research has shown that bereaved people take features of their lost loved one into their own characters as a part of absorbing grief. A wife who has always been absent-minded might inherit a husband's practicality. Some people take on the mannerisms and speech forms of their dead partner.

Personality changes sometimes mean that we develop more like our parent than we might have thought possible. Many people grow more like their parents with age. A common example of this is women who find themselves sounding just like their mothers when talking with their own children.

Sometimes losing a parent leaves the child with a sense of purpose, a determination that, even if parents appear to have achieved little in their lives, all shall not be lost or forgotten.

꒰ Michael had always been told how much he was like his father in looks and personality. To some extent he resented this, thinking it robbed him of his own identity. Initially devastated after his father died, Michael was pleased to realize that he had a lot of his father's easily offended character.

(Continued . . .)

And he had many of his father's mannerisms,
such as how he shut the door and whistled. He took
pride in his father's rugged individuality. He was
determined that what many saw as an obstinately
wasted life was not lived in vain.

To some extent, this involved a choice on Michael's part. A
choice is also involved in *rejecting* similarities. This doesn't mean
reacting against them, but deciding in your own way between
family characteristics and your own individuality.

Catching Up with Your Parent

Remember that you are living your *own* life and not performing
some play you inherited. We often measure ourselves and our
accomplishments against those of our parents, especially when we

> *Remember that you are living your own life and not performing some play you inherited.*

find ourselves surpassing goals they
never quite managed to reach. This kind
of intergeneration competitiveness is
subtle and pervasive and can even color
our own achievements.

Susan was delighted when she became a doctor
and over the years built up a successful general
practice. But satisfaction in her work was slightly
tinged with guilt because her father's own ambition
to be a doctor was not realized. She occasionally felt
resentful that she might be living out his life for
him, even though she enjoyed her work.
While deep down she was overjoyed with her
success, she felt the ambition she might have
inherited from her father always prevented her
from considering other options or living her life
in some other way.

This story illustrates how a parent can continue to dominate
your life even after death: You may have to come to terms with
inherited plans, a further maturing that entails separating your aims
from those of your parents. Realizing your comparative lack of

freedom, writing it down and talking about it with someone you trust are all first steps toward doing something you want to do.

You may feel an urge to do better than your parents, to be a better parent when raising your own children. Or you may be determined to avoid the mistakes that you know your parents made. This perception, however, will probably change along with your own circumstances.

> ✺ Maria always thought her mother had been wrong to give up her career to take care of her family. She thought her mother was bored and dissatisfied and that these feelings might have contributed to the eventual development of her illness. When Maria had a baby of her own, she realized the choice wasn't that easy, especially in her mother's time when it had been more accepted to stay at home. Maria compromised by working part-time in a local nursery.

Research has shown that as people grow older and approach the age at which their parent died, they often suffer a major life crisis or breakdown. Maybe they feel a lurking superstition that they too might die at that age. You might carry fears of dying the same way your parents did.

Depending on how they died—disease or accident—you can only take care of yourself as best you can. Otherwise, simply accepting your vulnerability is part of coming to terms with your own mortality.

Choosing a Partner

Unless a relationship is well established, there can be a danger in marrying too soon after a parent's death. Even apart from the temptation to find a substitute parent in a partner, it's easy to be attracted to anything that promises an escape from grief. The excitement of a love affair can be a distraction, but embarking on something that demands such long-term energy can be a mistake.

The relationship is likely to remain superficial because you are still absorbed with the process of grief and aren't yet free to love.

There are exceptions, of course. But even if you do meet the right person, chances are that it will be a quiet courtship, at least at first.

Part of finding a partner is the ritual of introducing him or her to your parents. This is a time when you may feel your loss again, especially if you feel that your father or mother would have been happy with your choice. When it's your turn to be introduced, it is easy to have high expectations of your in-laws in the unconscious hope that they will help replace the parents you have lost.

> ⟨ Heather was ready to see all sorts of good points in Will's father, although Will and he didn't actually get along that well. After a couple of years, Heather could admit her own feelings of dislike for Will's father and could see that he was not another version of her own father.

Your sense of loss can be compounded by envy of your partner if he or she still has parents. Perhaps you feel that your partner can't fully understand your loss. You may be impatient with your partner for complaining about minor failings in his or her own parents or for being on bad terms with them. After all, your partner's parents are still alive!

It is important to voice these feelings and equally important to try to talk yourself out of insisting that your other half understand *everything* you've been through. Communication can help bridge many gaps in understanding.

Becoming a Parent

Having children of your own profoundly alters your entire relationship with your parents. Suddenly you understand a lot more about why and how they did certain things with you as a child.

Having children of your own profoundly alters your entire relationship with your parents.

One part of becoming a parent, especially at first for women who have lost their mothers, is acknowledging the disappointment of not having your own parents around. This is a time when you need family support.

A new mother needs mothering. You may want to ask your mother all kinds of questions about how she handled her babies, from breastfeeding to babysitting. You may resent not having this practical and emotional support, particularly if your mother died just before the birth.

> ⚜ Michelle's mother died on the day she found out she was pregnant, depriving Michelle of future help. Michelle expressed her grief as resentment that there would be no one to babysit.

It isn't just a question of having a doting babysitter available—although it is much easier to leave children with a babysitter you know will enjoy them. It's having that kind of support standing by to help with this demanding new role. There may be a fantasy element in all this.

It is possible to be sentimental and forget that your mother might have been too occupied with her own life to babysit very often. Or she may have been unaware of your own needs for attention with a new baby. Or perhaps she would not be as uncritical or supportive as you would have liked!

It is true that having a baby can bring a resurgence of grief and you may miss your mother badly, even if she died several years before. You may also envy friends whose mothers come over immediately after the birth to see their daughters through the first few weeks, or take the children away for an occasional weekend.

You may regret that your own children are missing a valuable relationship because grandparents and grandchildren can form special bonds. However, their true emotional security comes from you, their own parents. You can always make the most of any other family members, such as your own brothers and sisters.

There is also the fact that, without your own parents around, you are free to put your own ideas into practice. You may gain independence and confidence more quickly through sheer necessity.

Some of your friends are going to have to explain the death of a grandparent to a child who came to know and love that person. That can be a lot harder than it is with a person the child has never known. Dealing with the absent grandparent can still be painful, especially when children are very young and don't have any understanding of time.

> ⚩ Maria's little boy, when he was three or four, electrified one family lunch by asking, "But Mommy, when you were a little girl, who was the mommy?" He then wanted to know where the mommy was now, what her name was and where he had been during all this.

Hard to answer! Luckily, small children are quite content with simple answers, such as your parent became very tired and went to a special place when the child himself was inside your tummy as a tiny baby. Be prepared for curiosity about dead grandparents, though. After all, it is part of their family history. A photo album and a few simple explanations can satisfy children who want to know more.

Children are a link with your parents.

Children are a link with your parents. They may resemble them physically or in mannerisms—the same color hair or eyes, a similar way of smiling or glancing that you can see while retaining your appreciation of each child as an individual.

Do We Ever Completely Accept Their Death?

Without a full understanding of what death is, it can be hard to accept that your parent isn't actually alive, even years later. It is difficult for the human mind to face the concept of death, of non-existence.

> ⚩ When Maria's mother had been dead for ten years, Maria started having fantasies that she had in fact been alive all this time in some other remote part of the world, some unknown town in Australia. Or she had divorced her father and was happily remarried and wasn't concerned about what her original family might be doing.

This sometimes happened when she saw a person who resembled her mother. These odd, drifting thoughts were also reinforced by dreams during sleep.

We never completely accept a mother's or father's death. Depending on your beliefs, you might also have a picture of your mother or father continuing to exist in some form in the afterlife. This too can be tinged with lingering resentment or sadness at being left for this other form of life.

Considering how desolate you feel at first, it is surprising how much you can accept what has happened. Life sweeps you on, with all its compelling needs—to earn a living, to bring up your own children. It is hard to remain completely swallowed up by grief when faced with this month's mortgage payment.

> *It is hard to remain completely swallowed up by grief when faced with this month's mortgage payment.*

Is There Any Value in Losing a Parent?

Nothing grates more on the recently bereaved's nerves than glib talk of the ultimate *value* of suffering. As one hospital chaplain pointed out, a parent's death can be looked at in two ways: The longer you have your parents, the luckier you are, but you are also unlucky because you haven't experienced what it's like *not* to have them.

You must confront that difficult question of the *value* of death. Perhaps it is more appropriate to talk in terms of *meaning* rather than value. This can mean altering your own values radically, perhaps redefining the idea of achievement in terms of what your parents really achieved in life.

If you always thought a career was extremely important, you may have to accept that a parent who died after a quiet stay-at-home life still enjoyed a vital life. It can take time to broaden your values this way, especially if you're involved in some activity your parents never engaged in.

Losing a parent means losing a friend, not just someone we have been dependent on. We may not realize just how much growing up we have to do until our parents die. Growing up and becoming adults to replace those we have lost is perhaps one of the best long-term tributes we can pay them.

Further Reading and Useful Addresses

On Losing a Parent

Akner, Lois F., and Catherine Whitney. *How to Survive the Loss of a Parent: A Guide for Adults*. New York: Quill, 1994.

Angel, Marc D. *The Orphaned Adult: Confronting the Death of a Parent*. Northvale, N.J.: Jason Aronson, 1997.

Becker, Marilyn R. *Last Touch: Preparing for a Parent's Death*. Oakland, Calif.: New Harbinger Publications, 1992.

Donnelly, Katherine F. *Recovering from the Loss of a Parent*. New York: Berkley Publishing Group, 1994.

Kennedy, Alexandra. *Losing a Parent: Passage to a New Way of Living*. San Francisco: Harper San Francisco, 1991.

Myers, Edward. *When Parents Die: A Guide for Adults*. New York: Penguin USA, 1997.

General Readings

Brooks, Anne M. *The Grieving Time: A Year's Account of Recovery from Loss*. New York: Herodias, 1999.

Carroll, David. *Living with Dying: A Loving Guide for Family and Close Friends*. St. Paul, Minn.: Paragon House Publishers, 1991.

Colgrove, Melba, Harold Bloomfield, and Peter McWilliams. *How to Survive the Loss of a Love*. Los Angeles: Prelude Press, 1993.

de Beauvoir, Simone. *A Very Easy Death*. New York: Pantheon Books, 1985.

Deits, Bob. *Life After Loss: A Personal Guide Dealing with Death, Divorce, Job Change and Relocation*. Fisher Books, 1999.

Grollman, Earl A. *Time Remembered: A Journal for Survivors*. Boston: Beacon Press, 1987.

———, ed. *What Helped Me When My Loved One Died*. Boston: Beacon Press, 1982.

James, John W., and Russel Friedman. *The Grief Recovery Handbook: The Action Program for Moving Beyond Death, Divorce, and Other Losses*. New York: HarperCollins Publishers, 1998.

Kübler-Ross, Elisabeth. *On Life after Death*. Berkeley, Calif.: Celestial Arts Publishing Co., 1991.

———, ed. *Death: The Final Stage of Growth.* New York: Simon & Schuster, 1997.

Levine, Stephen. *Healing into Life and Death.* New York: Anchor Books, 1989.

Lewis C.S. *A Grief Observed.* San Francisco: Harper San Francisco, 1995.

Lightner, Candy. *Giving Sorrow Words: How to Cope with Grief & Get on with Your Life.* New York: Warner Books, Inc., 1991.

O'Connor, Nancy. *Letting Go with Love: The Grieving Process.* Tucson, Ariz.: La Mariposa Press, 1994.

Rando, Therese A., Ph.D. *How to Go on Living When Someone You Love Dies.* New York: Bantam Books, Inc., 1991.

Schiff, Harriet S. *Living Through Mourning: Finding Comfort and Hope When a Loved One Has Died.* New York: Viking Penguin, 1987.

Staudacher, Carol. *Men & Grief.* Oakland, Calif.: New Harbinger Publications, 1991.

Tatelbaum, Judy. *The Courage to Grieve: Create Living, Recovery, & Growth Through Grief.* New York: HarperCollins Publishers, 1984.

Temes, Roberta. *Living with an Empty Chair: A Guide Through Grief.* Far Hills, N.J.: New Horizon Press Publishers, Inc., 1992.

Vail, Elaine. *A Personal Guide to Living with Loss.* New York: Wiley, 1982.

Viorst, Judith. *Necessary Losses.* New York: Fireside, 1998.

Walsh, Froma, and Monica McGoldrick, eds. *Living Beyond Loss: Death in the Family.* New York: W.W. Norton & Co., 1995.

Professionals/Counselors

Furman, Erna, and Anna Freud, eds. *A Child's Parent Dies: Studies in Childhood Bereavement.* New Haven, Conn.: Yale University Press, 1981.

Piper, William E., Mary McCallum, Hassan F. Azim. *Adaptation to Loss Through Short-Term Group Psychotherapy.* New York: Guilford Press, 1999.

Worden, J. William. *Grief Counseling & Grief Therapy: A Handbook for the Mental Health Practitioner.* New York: Springer Publishing Co., Inc., 1991.

For Children

Bratman, Fred. *Everything You Need to Know When a Parent Dies.* New York: Rosen Publishing Group, 1998.

Mellonie, Bryan, and Robert Ingpen. *Lifetimes: The Beautiful Way to Explain Death to Children*. New York: Bantam Doubleday Dell, 1987.

Silverstein, Shel. *Giving Tree*. New York: HarperCollins Children's Books, 1964.

Temes, Roberta. *The Empty Place: A Child's Guide Through Grief*. Far Hills, N.J.: New Horizon Press Publishers, Inc., 1992.

Suicide

Humphry, Derek. *Final Exit*. New York: Dell Publishing Co., Inc., 1992.

Rollin, Betty. *Last Wish*. New York: Warner Books, Inc., 1986.

Smolin, Ann, and John Guinan. *Healing after the Suicide of a Loved One*. New York: Simon & Schuster Trade, 1993.

Hospice/Dying at Home

Beresford, Larry. *The Hospice Handbook: A Complete Guide*. Boston: Little, Brown & Co., 1993.

Callanan, Maggie, and Patricia Kelley. *Final Gifts: Understanding the Special Awareness, Needs and Communications of the Dying*. New York: Poseidon/Simon & Schuster, 1992.

Hayslip, Bert. *Hospice Care*. Newbury Park, Calif.: Sage Publications, Inc., 1992.

Sankar, Andrea. *Dying at Home: A Family Guide for Caregiving*. Baltimore: Johns Hopkins, 1991.

Funeral Planning

Morgan, Ernest. *Dealing Creatively with Death: A Manual of Death Education and Simple Burial*. Bayside, N.Y.: Barclay House Books, 1998.

Nissley, Julia. *How to Probate an Estate*. Berkeley, Calif.: Nolo.com, 1999.

Sublette, Kathleen, and Martin Flagg. *Final Celebrations: A Guide for Personal and Family Funeral Planning*. Ventura: Pathfinder Publishing of California, 1992.

Aging

CAPS (Children of Aging Parents)
1609 Woodbourne Rd., #302A
Levittown, PA 19057
800-227-7294
Website: www.careguide.net/
careguide.cgi/caps/capshome.
html

Concerned Relatives of
Nursing Home Patients
3130 Mayfield Rd., Ste. 209W
Cleveland Heights, OH 44118
216-321-0403

Area 10 Agency on Aging
2129 Yost Ave.
Bloomington, IN 47401
812-334-3383

Bereavement Organizations

Bereaved Families of Ontario
562 Eglinton Ave. E., Ste. 401
Toronto, ON M4P 1P1
416-440-0290
Fax: 416-440-0304
Website: www.inforamp.net/~bfo/
index.html
*Website lists affiliates throughout
Canada*

Bereavement Support
Services—Canada
905-628-6008

Grief Recovery Hotline
800-445-4808

The International THEOS
Foundation
322 Blvd. of the Allies, Ste. 105
Pittsburgh, PA 15222-1919
412-471-7779
Fax: 412-471-7782

Widowed Persons Service
c/o AARP
601 E St. NW
Washington, DC 20049
202-434-2260

Death Education and Research

ADEC (Association for Death
Education and Counseling)
638 Prospect Ave.
Hartford, CT 06105-4298
860-586-7503
Website: www.adec.org/

International Institute for the
Study of Death
P.O. Box 63026
Miami, FL 33163-0026
305-936-1408

Hospices/Dying at Home

B.C. Hospice Palliative Care
Association
Room 502, Comox Bldg.
1081 Burrard St.
Vancouver, BC V6Z 1Y6
604-631-5821
Fax: 604-631-5822

Canadian Palliative Care Association
286, 48 Bruyere St.
Ottawa, ON I1N 5C8
800-668-2785
Fax: 613-562-4226

Hospice & Palliative Care Manitoba
2109 Portage Ave.
Winnipeg, MB R3J 0L3
204-889-8525
Fax: 204-888-8874

Hospice Association of Ontario
40 Wynford Dr., Ste. 313
Don Mills, ON M3C 1J5
416-510-3880
Fax: 416-510-3882

HospiceLink
800-331-1620
Website: nysernet.org/bcic/
numbers/hospice.html
Referral and information program

Island Hospice Association
c/o Prince Edward Home
5 Brighton Rd.
Charlottetown, PE C1A 8T6
902-368-4498
Fax: 902-368-5946

National Hospice Organization
1901 N. Moore St., Ste. 901
Arlington, VA 22209
800-658-8898
Fax: 703-525-5762
Website: www.nho.org

New Brunswick Palliative Care
Association
c/o Regional Hospital Centre
1750 Sunset Dr.
Bathurst, NB E2A 4L7
506-548-8961
Fax: 506-545-2440

Nova Scotia Hospice/Palliative Care
Association
c/o Northwood Care Inc.
2615 Northwood Terrace
Halifax, NS B3K 3S5
902-454-3312
Fax: 902-455-6408

Palliative Care Association of Alberta
Box 3020
Stony Plain, AB T7Z 1Y4
403-963-4453
Fax: 403-963-0161

Saskatchewan Palliative Care
Association
230 Ave. R South, Ste. 111
Saskatoon, SK S7K 2Z1
306-382-2550
Fax: 306-382-3448

University of Ottawa Institute of
Palliative Care
SCO Hospital
43 Bruyere St.
Ottawa, ON K1N 5C8
613-562-6301
Fax: 613-562-4226
Website: www.pallcare.org

Illness

ADRDA (Alzheimer's Disease and
Related Disorders Association, Inc.)
919 N. Michigan Ave., #1100
Chicago, IL 60611
800-272-3900, 312-853-3060

Alzheimer's Society of Canada
20 Eglinton Ave. West, Ste. 1200
Toronto, ON M4R 1K8
800-616-8816

American Cancer Society
19 W. 56th St.
New York, NY 10019
212-586-8700

American Institute of Life-
Threatening Illness and Loss
(Division of Foundation of
Thanatology)
630 W. 168th St.
New York, NY 10032
914-779-4877
Fax: 914-793-0813
Website: www.lifethreat.org/

Cancer Hotline Information Service
(U.S.)
800-4CANCERS

Cancer Information Service
(Canada)
800-263-6750

HOPE Center for Cancer Support
297 Wickenden St.
Providence, RI 02903
401-454-0404
Fax: 401-454-0411
Website: www.hopecenter.net/
vol.htm

Leukemia Research Fund
1110 Finch Ave. W., Ste. 220
Toronto, ON M3J 2T2
800-268-2144

Leukemia Society of America
600 3rd Ave.
New York, NY 10016
212-573-8484, 800-284-4271

National Coalition for Cancer
Survivorship
1010 Wayne Ave.
Silver Spring, MD 20910
301-650-8868

Suicide and Right to Die Organizations

American Association of
Suicidology
4201 Connecticut Ave. NW, Ste. 408
Washington, DC 20008
202-237-2280
Fax: 202-237-2282
Website: www.suicidology.org/
   index.html
*Click on National Directory for
list of local groups in United States
and Canada*

Choice in Dying
1035 Thirtieth St. NW
Washington, DC 20007
800-989-WILL
Website: www.choices.org

Compassion in Dying Federation
PMB 415
6312 Southwest Capitol Highway
Portland, OR 97201
503-221-9556
Fax: 503-228-9160
Website: www.compassionindying.
   org/

Dying with Dignity
55 Eglinton Ave. E.
Toronto, ON M4P 1G8
800-495-6156

Euthanasia Research and Guidance
Organization (ERGO)
24829 Norris Ln.
Junction City, OR 97448-9559
541-998-1873
Website: www.finalexit.org/

The Hemlock Society
P.O. Box 101810
Denver, CO 80250-1810
800-247-7421
Fax: 303-639-1224
Website: www.hemlock.org/
   hemlock/about_hemlock.htm

SAFER (Suicide Attempt, Follow-up,
Education, Research)
300-2425 Quebec St.
Vancouver, BC V5T 4L6
604-879-9251

Suicide Information and Education
Centre (SIEC)
201-1615 10th Ave. SW
Calgary, Alberta, T3C 0J7
403-245-3900
Fax: 403-245-0299
Website: www.siec.ca

Index